LEAD ME LORD

A Journey of Trust and Hope

Pam Lile

ISBN 978-1-63630-029-0 (Paperback)
ISBN 978-1-63630-030-6 (Digital)

Covenant Books, Inc.
11661 Hwy 707
Murrells Inlet, SC 29576
www.covenantbooks.com

CONTENTS

PREFACE

A few months had passed since Sam's stroke. As I was contemplating a prompting that I had to put our story down on paper, I recalled an instance a few months prior to that fateful day when I had met a friend for coffee. We were enjoying a conversation concerning our gifts, our callings, our work to do in this life. I admitted to her that I knew what my calling was. But I felt rather inept at the work. My heart was designed to welcome souls into this world, and though I tried my best, I just couldn't seem to go to sleep at night confident that I was meeting all of their needs. My lofty aspirations were continually at odds with my ability to accomplish even the first thing. At the end of the day, my list of accomplishments was short while my unfinished business grew exponentially.

Additionally, we had purchased a small business a few years prior. It was a lovely little educational supply store which we felt inspired to purchase. Prayerfully, we went into the venture as a family. Indeed, we had some good times there. The children all received a pretty good education on entrepreneurship and customer service. Many lessons were learned as they greeted customers and commanded the cash register for purchases. They all felt quite grown up and important. Our staff was amazing, our customers inspiring, and the merchandise—well, a Garden of Eden for a homeschool family. The allure languished, however, as we tried to balance work and school. I was leaving the kids home more and more so that they could attend to their studies. Eventually, I brought my office home so that I did not need to leave them more than absolutely necessary.

As time went by, it turned into a business that was being run from home, and I lost the ambition for the work. It became Quickbooks and payroll, taxes and scheduling. The "fun" of running the store was gone, and I was left with the mundane work of keeping it afloat behind the scenes. My sense of purpose in the venture was fading, and a weary spirit was setting in as I struggled to understand whether or not we were still in the center of God's will. The time spent running the store contributed, of course, to my growing list of household goals that remained unfinished at the end of the day. Without a sense of purpose in the work, all I could see was a distraction from the work God was calling me to at home.

Following this conversation with my friend, I was lamenting that I couldn't put my finger on my *gift*. My calling…no problem. I was called to be a mom. But my gift—that seemed to be a whole other question indeed. I was languishing in my role as a store owner and felt incompetent in my responsibilities as a mother. I was lacking something that I was passionate about and talented in. I had the sense that if I could find my passion, then my finger would be on my gift. As I drove home that night, I was pondering all these things. Pulling down my road, I began to utter a simple question. Before I could even get the entire thought out, an answer was already in my mind. "Lord, where do you want me to focus my energy? What is my talent? What is my gift?"

"You will write" was the reply.

I have had conversations like this before. A thought that comes from outside of yourself. A thought that catches you by surprise. A thought that finds a home in your soul the second it lands. *Huh*, I thought. *I do enjoy writing. But what on earth would I write about, and who would want to read it anyway?* Additionally, I contemplated that writing would take *time*—a commodity we were running short on as it was. I put the thought in my back pocket to ponder again at a later date.

Little did I know that God was already writing a story that was more wonderfully captivating and awe-inspiring than I could imagine. Those are not the words that I would have chosen initially. But in hindsight, the story really is quite amazing.

In our story, Sam spent seventy-three days at Akron Children's Hospital. From his bedside, I would pour my heart out on his Facebook page, keeping everyone updated on his progress, begging prayers, bringing the world along on our journey. Occasionally, a kind soul would offer a compliment on my perceived literary skills. Each time my writing caught the attention of another, I would pull that thought out of my pocket and consider that *this* is what He wants me to write about. Eventually, my writing caught the attention of an influential speaker and radio personality from our area who asked me to contribute a reflection to a book she was compiling with many different authors. Graciously, I accepted and was thrilled to see our story in print. I was not thrilled in the sense that it stroked my ego but rather because the road we were traveling was damn hard! To see your story in print somehow anchors your experience in time for the world to learn about. It is now documented that we went through this very difficult thing, and now the world will have a record of it. And if it says so in print and others are willing to read it, then it *must* have a purpose. The fact that others would have an interest in reading our story meant that our suffering wasn't in vain. Our suffering was having an impact on our small portion of the world. To see God's hand and to *share* God's hand with others was balm for my weary spirit. Our heavy, heavy cross had a purpose. And I could see a small glimpse of that purpose in the hearts that were touched.

As I contemplated writing this book, a sinister voice would inevitably turn up masked as the voice of reason. What on earth would I say? My own thoughts and feelings were still a jumbled mess, and somehow, I was supposed to put them down on paper in some sort of organized fashion that would touch the hearts of others. Would others perceive a book such as this as a mom exploiting her son's tragedy in the pursuit of getting published? Would they understand my heart? I was nearly ready to put the idea to bed for a while as I really didn't have any clear direction. I considered that perhaps now was not the right time. But then a gentle thought—again out of the blue, again connecting as it landed.

"This is my story. I am the one writing it. You only need to put it down on paper. Just tell the story."

That thought stayed with me as I took Sam into the hospital for his therapy that day. Coincidentally, I met a lovely mother for the first time who I had heard so much about. She was with her daughter; their deep wound still very fresh as tears filled the eyes of this lovely lady. In our brief encounter, she sighed, "But we are a hope-filled people. And God writes the best stories."

Indeed, He does. And occasionally, He asks us to write them down. I had my assignment.

It had a curious beginning, this book. I began writing without knowing the ending. I began writing with jumbled thoughts and without a clear sense of purpose. I began writing on the edge of my seat just waiting to hear how it ended! Whenever I began to wonder what Sam's outcome would ultimately be, I found myself turning to writing. If I could do the work of telling our story up until now, then I would be ready when the next chapter presented itself.

Our journeys are all so very unique. God deals with each soul in a way that perfectly complements their design. Our journey, our cross, was custom made for our family. But I have learned that the cross is to be shared. The journey is to be shared. The lessons are to be shared. We have been on Calvary. We have been at the foot of the cross. We have been Simon carrying the cross. We have been the Israelites wandering in exile. We have been Joseph awaiting the fulfillment of the promise that was made to him. We have been Abraham offering his son. We have been in the fiery furnace. And we have been at the empty tomb. And in each and every circumstance, we have traveled with the Body of Christ. Everyone that surrounded us, those who prayed for us and with us, they all took part in our suffering and in our joy. They took part in our *story*! This story is not just about a boy and his family. It is about an entire community of believers united in heart and soul, connected to each other through the story that God is writing, changing the world through our interaction. And yes, at the center of the story is one very special boy. Sam.

Samuel = God has heard.

CHAPTER 1

A Painful Paradise

Something is not as I remember it in sunny Davenport Florida. Every fiber of my being recognizes this place that I am in. I have been here before and have watched my children play in *this* water. I have felt *this* sunshine and allowed *this* breeze to console my winter-weary soul on numerous occasions. I have heard *these* squeals of delight from children running and playing every year for much of my adult life. Yes, this is a safe memory—a time and place of carefree bliss away from the bustle of everyday life, a memory that I have had the pleasure of reliving each winter. As my senses try desperately to settle into this safe memory of mine, to get comfortable in a time and place from my past that beckons me to lay my burdens down, I am met with the harsh reality of a new dynamic. There is a reality this year that grates agonizingly in the wrong direction. This change, this different, this difficult—it has followed us here to Florida. This is the reason for my tears. Something is not as I remember it. On the surface, this oasis remains unchanged, but upon closer examination, it is clear that the Florida Liles of 2019 are a different kind of family than the one who came in 2018. *Everything* is different since Sam's stroke and vacation is no exception. This reality has the ability to draw tears from my unsuspecting eyes without even a conscious thought in my head as to why.

In my mind's eye, I see my eight-year-old boy scurrying around the bend just long enough to call out that he's running up to the top pool to swim.

"One minute, Sam!" I beckon. "You'll need your sunscreen before you get wet!"

Sam obediently skips over to get slathered before running to the pool so as not to miss out on a single minute of fun. This kid in my mind is all play. All spunk. All adventure. My spirit wrestles with this sun-speckled, happy thought. It's hard to say if this memory is trying to console me or taunt me. Happy Sam? Not so much this year. Instead, I turn around to find that same boy sitting on a lounge chair in his leg brace and the sweatpants that we couldn't talk him out of despite our greatest attempts at cajoling and reasoning.

"But Sam, you are going to be so hot in your long pants! Why not just put some shorts on? Or better yet, your swim trunks *just in case* you change your mind." Sam has no patience for reason or persuasion or even fun this year. He just feels how he feels. He has no interest in swimming or doing any other such activity. He groans in the heat but has no desire to cool off in the pool. He can't really even express the reason why he is so resistant to play and fun, he just doesn't want to. The handful of victories that we celebrated in leading him to the water were dampened by his painful attempt at walking on his spastic bare foot without his brace. Dampened by urgent trips to the bathroom as we rush him out of the pool and sling all ninety wet pounds of him on our backs to carry him because he is incapable of making these trips on his own. Dampened by the occasional outburst of emotion as he sits and sobs with an audible groan indifferent to the eyes staring nervously at him. Yes, this boy is much different than the one who exists in the safe harbor of my memories—and that is the cause of my grief. I miss my boy. Oh, how desperately I miss him.

This vacation is one more experience among many that tugs at my heart and forces it to detach once again from what was, to settle into what is. Will we ever feel normal again? Will we merely survive this ordeal but never again flourish? Will our family ever dance again?

The thoughts and memories of "what was" come crashing down on me with a new vigor.

This is not the first time I've wrestled with the unexpected arrival of grief. Merely being in our home causes my heart to wince in pain. As I look around our familiar surroundings, I see my Sam everywhere! I see him skip around the corner. I watch him whistle as he washes the dishes with his huge yellow gloves covering two able hands. I see him playing with his little brother with a maturity that is admirable. In my mind, he is patient and generous—capable of sharing, capable of being the big brother and doing all those important things that big brothers do. Every turn of my head in our home is a painful wound inflicted on my consciousness. Watching the kids run around outside without the one who would have done it longest and best has caused my breath to catch in my throat more times than I can count. I am brought to my knees by photographs of years past. Anything familiar that forces me to come to terms with what was lost is like a lashing that takes a pound of flesh, and this vacation was no exception. It is different. And different is hard. Instead of my happy, fun-loving, adventurous little guy, I find myself caught unaware over and over again by this nine-year-old boy who has the patience of a two-year-old and moves as if he were ninety.

The frequency with which thoughts of our past strike like lightning is increasing. It has been eight months since I last saw the boy from my memories. The running, skipping, carefree play. His smile, enthusiasm, and boyish qualities. His quick processing speed, his love of working alongside his dad, his picnics, and attention to detail in setting up a fine dining environment. His red wagon full of goodies that runs along behind him through the yard. His love of bonfires and tents and *life*! All of these memories from my past are slipping away. My brain can sense that they are being lost and replaced with this new personality. This flat personality that does not enjoy play. In a last-ditch desperate attempt to remember all the quirks that I loved most about my son, lest they be lost and replaced forever, my mind is protecting those memories by bringing them to the forefront of my attention when I least expect it. The more I resist going down that painful road willingly, either through my conscious thoughts or deliberate strolls through photographs, the more my mind forces it upon me. As much as it hurts, I'm grateful for the intrusions. As much as I don't want to look, I equally don't want to forget.

Grief can be such a complicated emotion. I am grieving what we went through. And though grateful for how far we have come, grieving what we are still going through. I'm grieving time lost and our "new normal"—a term I loathe with every ounce of my being. I miss the gift of an ordinary day. I am grieving the loss of Sam as I knew him. I'm grieving our carefree existence as I knew it, grieving the skip, the hop, the jump, and the climb that died that day. The eight-year-old bare foot that went into hiding inside a plastic prison, never again to be seen by the light of day. I'm grieving the fact that I didn't soak up every tiny little moment knowing our life as we knew it was going to come to a screeching halt. And I am lamenting that in the busyness that we now find ourselves, I *still* don't soak it up as I should. There is laundry and dishes and school and therapy after all. Children to dress and feed and keep clean. How do you pause to soak up the best of your days when things come crashing down if you stop for a moment?

But, as I said, it's complicated. Sam is still with us. I continue to adore him every bit as much as I did before. I can't really grieve the loss of Sam because he is still here with us! He remembers us. He remembers *everything*—praise God! I even catch glimpses of his old idiosyncrasies that defined him from time to time. While I grieve what we lost, there is still the hope that it will be restored. And so, I can't really grieve it as something lost for good. There is still healing that can happen, and with healing comes restoration. And with restoration comes more of what we once thought to be lost forever. And so, I don't allow grief to set up camp because I realize that it is a temporary loss to some degree, and ultimately God will decide what we need to bid farewell to permanently, if anything. And if that time should come, He will give me the grace to accept it.

I attempt to push all negative thoughts far from my mind. We are after all on a lovely, much-needed family vacation. The past eight months have been spent in the cold sterile environment of a hospital separated from one another for much of that time. I know the dangers of wallowing in self-pity, of staying in a spirit of defeat and ingratitude for how far we have come from the day of Sam's stroke. I could very easily waste this precious time with my family in a wrong frame of mind that would cripple me for the duration of our stay. And so I allow a few tears to escape to console my broken heart. But then I dry my eyes, turn around, and allow God to hold me once again as I soldier on with all the trust I can muster. I allow my mind to return down the path from which we came. The path on which my God has made himself manifest at every turn. It is by looking back that I can move forward. I know where I have been, and so I can have confidence in where I am going. But I don't just go back to the day of the stroke. I allow myself to go even further. My mind wanders back in time to a day about four years ago—the day I entered into a dance with my God, the day when He called me into a conversation that left me forever changed and prepared my heart for the trials that awaited me.

CHAPTER 2

Beckoned

We were a busy but happy household. While we had lived on our three acres for around three years now, we had only recently settled into the new house that my husband and his dad had built for us next door to the small basement that we had called home for a while. Though modest in size, it seemed like a large space compared to what we had just moved out of. It was a lovely summer day—not too hot. The kids were enjoying one of those moments that only fresh air and exercise can bring when not a soul was at odds with another. Their laughter and play found its way to my ears and brought joy to my soul. I seized upon my opportunity, grabbed all of my gardening supplies, novice though I was, and stepped outside to put in a bit of time in my vegetable patch. Admittedly, I was much better at cultivating weeds than anything edible, but I didn't have enough sense to be discouraged just yet.

As I stepped outside my back door to begin my stroll to the garden, I found myself suddenly stopped in my tracks. I gazed across the expanse of our property and felt incredibly overwhelmed by it. Suddenly everything appeared wild and unruly—a beast of a property that could not be tamed. What had, until that moment, seemed like quite a lovely thing all full of promise and potential was now threatening and ominous to my eyes. It was almost closing in upon me and choking me. This took me by surprise, of course, but the emotion that followed was doubly curious. In the blink of an eye, I became incredibly homesick specifically for a house that we had lived in years before—a house that I hadn't given a second thought to for many years. The very thought of this house brought with it a literal ache that set up camp within me.

These thoughts and emotions did not seem to develop from my mind the way a thought typically does. Typically, one thought leads to another to another to another, and you can trace the lineage of how you came to think that thought. These thoughts were different. Almost as if another had dropped them randomly in my brain to confound me. I was startled by them as they seemed to be from outside of myself, and yet my soul instantly took ownership of them as soon as they landed. I stood thinking, processing, for what seemed an eternity but was likely only a minute or so. In an instant, my home environment became overwhelming, and my heart longed for another space—a specific space known to us as Tisdale.

What is wrong with me! I thought. *Will I never be satisfied? Dave and Paul just finished building a good solid home on a beautiful piece of land! We just moved in a few months prior. What can I be thinking to have such a desire to move again?* Convinced that this was a personality flaw that needed to be reasoned with, I went inside to find something to give me a swift kick in the pants after a half-hearted go in the garden. My Bible wasn't where I usually kept it, though I wasn't really in the habit of reading it consistently anyway. I found *The Imitation of Christ* by Thomas A. Kempis instead.

Aha! I thought. *I'll look in here for something concerning the desires of my heart so that, together, Kempis and I can root out whatever sinful nature I'm wrestling with.* I was seeking something that would both convict and console me at the same time so that I could lay this thought to rest.

I did a quick search on the word *desire*, hoping to find something concerning inordinate desires. What happened next cannot be explained in the natural order of things. While that book is chock full of great advice, wisdom on picking up your cross and following Jesus, plentiful passages concerning inordinate desires and detachment from worldly things... I read *none* of that! What I read that day and over and over again in the days that followed—the passage that I can still picture in my mind's eye, the passage that I shared with my sisters in astonishment the next evening—it is no longer in this book of mine. I have devoured this little book from cover to cover, seeking to recover what first spoke to me only to come up empty-handed. What I read that night when I was feeling such a *desire to go home* was this: "I have placed these desires within your heart. Wait and see what I can do with them." Lest you think this passage a figment of my imagination, wishful thinking run amok, just stay with me as I take you deeper into this experience.

This passage caught in my throat. What are the chances that I would open to this beauty out of any other passage in the book? Still, I wasn't convinced. I acknowledged that God had my attention, but I still wrestled with whether it was all just a crazy coincidence. Could it be that I was seeking something to justify a desire that I had? I should probably dismiss that little passage for several reasons. First, Tisdale is no longer our home nor has it been our home for many years! Tisdale now belonged to another, and so even if I wanted to move back, it wasn't an option. Secondly, *why*? We had just built a lovely home on a beautiful piece of land. Why would I want to go back? The thought of that hypothetical conversation with my husband was enough to put this idea to bed: "Honey, I know that you just sacrificed a year of your life to build us a beautiful home and that we just moved in a few months ago. But I think God is calling us back to Tisdale—which, by the way, is not even for sale." No, I was fairly certain that this was all some kind of "grass is greener" syndrome that needed time to dissipate.

Instead of counting sheep that night, I lay in bed counting my blessings. I began thinking about all that I had to be grateful for. All the blessings of the home we lived in and the potential blessings that we were looking forward to in utilizing the land that we had at our disposal. Gardens and fruit trees, chickens and zip lines, patios and lounge chairs. There was so much to look forward to *here*! "Please, Lord," I pleaded. "Please take this desire away from me." This feeling of being homesick was so intense that it created a literal ache in my heart. As I practiced gratitude, I fell into a slumber fully expecting to feel better by morning.

As I roused myself from my sleep the following morning, I was disappointed to find that this desperate feeling remained. It pestered my consciousness all day. As we rounded the corner on that Sunday and settled into the early evening, Dave joined me by the small fire flickering in the makeshift ring in the backyard. As he casually sat down beside me, he unceremoniously announced, "You'll never guess who I talked to today!"

"Who?" I asked with half an interest, as my thoughts were elsewhere.

"Kevin from Tisdale. He said our old house is back on the market!" A jolt went through me as I came to understand what had just happened! My heart fluttered as a queasiness filled my stomach! "Did he really just say what I think he said? Good Lord, what are you trying to do here?" I couldn't quite get my thoughts together to even begin a conversation with Dave concerning all that was transpiring in my confounded mind, and so I simply said, "Oh, you're kidding me," with the tiny bit of composure at my disposal. A minute later, I announced that I would "be right back." I had to catch my breath. I needed something to affirm that I wasn't crazy. For the second time in two days, I headed inside to open my Bible; and for the second time in two days, it was not where it should have been. Little did I know at the time, but this was the beginning of a daily habit that would carry me through the next four years and beyond. This was the beginning of the journey that would lead me to thirst for that next conversation with God through His sacred Scriptures. But in this moment, my Bible could not be found. And so, I went back to Kempis. This time I opened up that gem of a book and found this.

Christ: My child, in every circumstance this is how you should pray: "Lord, if it be Your will, so let it be, and if it be to Your honor, let it be fulfilled in Your Name. Lord, if this be for my good, give me the grace to use it for Your honor; but if You know that it will be harmful to me and not profitable to my soul, then take away from me such a desire."

> *It is with fear of God, and a humble heart that you should desire and ask for whatever comes to your mind as desirable. With entire abandonment of yourself to God, commit all things to Me, saying: "Do with me what you know to be best, as pleases You best and as will best promote Your glory." (The Imitation of Christ)*

First, I ran to God. Once He had His say, I turned to my sisters invoking that brand of therapy that can be surprisingly effective even through the screen of your phone. "What in the world?!" I began. "I think I might be going crazy!" I began to recount the story of the past day and a half. They helped me to explore possible explanations for my homesick heart, explanations for the support I received from Thomas A. Kempis, but there was that pesky little detail of the amazing coincidental circumstances of Tisdale going back on the market at the exact same time. No amount of wishful thinking could have caused that to happen. This was big. And time would tell whether God was actually leading me somewhere.

I did not bring Dave into the conversation for quite a while. Mostly because I just didn't know how to bring it up! Any reasonable response from him would acknowledge the absurdity of moving out of a house we just moved into. I figured that this desire was placed in my heart by God, and so God would work it out somehow. I didn't understand it myself, and so how could I talk about it? Instead, I spent my time in conversation with God. *All day long*, I talked to God. This, too, was the beginning of a new habit! Daily conversation *with* God instead of merely praying *to* God. I was in my own head for much of the day, sizing up this journey that I was being called to, trying to understand how God works, sorting out what could be God speaking to me from what could be the devil tempting me. Indeed, I saw both at work. I learned what Lectio Divina was, and this discipline proved to be the single most effective tool in aiding my conversation with God. It was in running to Scripture daily that I came to realize that God had something unique and exciting to say that was meant for only me! I had heard that His Word was living, but I had always understood that to mean that it is relevant today just as it was thousands of years ago. What I didn't realize was that *this* is just the tip of the iceberg! By His word being *alive*, it means that it speaks directly to your heart, in your unique circumstances, penetrating to the very core of who you are! That is what it means to be alive! His Word is more alive than the person sitting next to you. And all this, I had to discover. You see, I was God's biggest fan! I knew all about Him! I even professed to believe in miracles and the power of prayer, though I had never really experienced it in a tangible way. At least not in a way that was big enough to fully relegate it to the realm of the miraculous. But in some measure, I did believe, and so I always had some kind of a relationship with God, anemic though it was.

But this was different. For all I knew, for the hundreds of hours that I had spent getting to know about my religion and to know about my God, I was lacking the most important piece. I was lacking a knowledge *of* my God. To know *about* God and to know God Himself are two entirely different concepts! By extending this invitation to me and drawing me to Himself and by my acceptance of this invitation, an entirely new relationship was formed! It was exciting! He was leading me as the Good Shepherd! Thoughts would enter my mind throughout the day concerning my journey. The ones that pestered me were the ones that I paid attention to. Sure enough, that thought that was rolling and swirling around in my head all day would be affirmed through my daily reading of Scripture. As I began to faithfully follow the readings of the daily Mass, I very quickly caught on to the idea that *this*—*this* is what it means that His Word is *alive!* What most people know as coincidences happened most days through the mingling of my own thoughts with the words in Scripture! Occasionally, His love notes would be sent to me through random conversations with people or the catchy signs that decorate the yards of various churches. A song that would come into my head and move this otherwise unemotional gal to tears. Often a homily would hit me right between the eyes or just a peaceful feeling with pins and needles that accompanied a certain good thought during my conversations with Him. Very often, I would meet God in nature. When I would find time to sit outdoors in solitude with my coffee and my Bible, soaking in His glorious creation, peace would flood my soul as I would listen in silence and let His thoughts become my thoughts.

At first, this new conversation often felt very much like wrestling. I was desperate to make heads or tails of where my thoughts and feelings and coincidences were coming from. But over time, this wrestle turned into a dance. I learned to let Him lead, and the motions of my soul became more and more graceful and peaceful. Occasionally, the dance would turn dramatic and restless. From time to time, I would push Him away by not trusting all I was experiencing. Every now and again, there would be a spiritual misstep by trying to predict where He was going to lead me next, causing the smooth transitions to become rough and labored, but my good God always called me back to rest in His arms and onward we would dance together. He would lead. I would follow.

Our relationship had grown stronger through *Lectio Divina*. Each day spoke of the journey. Often, it came through the Old Testament readings concerning the exile of the Israelites. These readings filled me with such joy to know that at some point God would make sense of all of it, and I too would be led to my promised land. So sure was I that we were being led back to Tisdale. After some time, though, it occurred to me that God seemed to be leading me on the journey to nowhere. We kept talking and talking…and talking some more. I was searching for God in every step of my day. And yet, nothing was *happening*.

After a couple of months, it occurred to me that perhaps God was asking me to do this very difficult thing of talking to my husband about this journey that I saw us on. I didn't know how I was to bring it up. What would I say? I decided to appeal to his logic, and so I was ready to spell out exactly how God had been speaking to me. How could he argue, after all, with that coincidental beginning when Tisdale went back on the market? But I needed more. I knew that wouldn't be enough, and so I threw in some tidbits to appeal to his sensible nature—about how we bought the property expecting to dabble in animal husbandry and gardening. We had dreamed of creating a little mini farm. And yet we were coming up short at every turn. We were tiring of the idea of farm animals when we came to the realization that they were more work than we had time, knowledge, or energy for. Additionally, we were discouraged by the pitiful crop that was enjoyed mostly by insects, deer, and blight. Indeed, this venture had not really proven to be all we hoped for, and so perhaps we were more suited for the suburbs. Yes, I was ready. Come, Holy Spirit, I'm ready to talk to my husband.

As gently as I could, I made my case. I admitted that I didn't understand the reason why, but I really felt that God was calling us back to Tisdale. I laid bare our miserable garden and canning failures, our dashed hopes and expectations of what was possible with all this land. His response? Exactly as you would expect a reasonable person to respond. What I was asking for was indeed ridiculous, and the absurdity was not lost on Dave. He concluded that I looked into things too deeply and that if I didn't want to garden, then I should just not garden. He wouldn't mind a bit if I gave up on that pipe dream as he realized the futility of tackling the seemingly impossible. After all, we did have a gaggle of small children and no knowledge or experience whatsoever in farming. This was nothing more than a tale of "I fought the weeds and the weeds won." And that was that. The conversation was over as fast as it began, and nowhere in it did I sense the presence of my God. It was awkward and painful and short and disconnected. I consoled myself with the thought that I had done my part in planting a seed that God could water and nurture. But time went by, and the conversation never came up again.

By mid-October, we received word that Tisdale had sold. My shoulders hung low that day as I tried to make sense of everything. Perhaps everything I thought I knew was wrong! Perhaps this dance was really just me dancing by myself. A figment of my imagination. Or worse yet.... Perhaps I was dancing with the devil and not even realizing it! How could this be? No. It wasn't my imagination! Even if all of my chats with God involved wishful thinking on my part, you still can't explain away the coincidence that started it all! My dancing went back to wrestling as I felt a bit let down by my God. It was a heavy blow. I still longed to go home, and now I felt that my God had abandoned me. He led my heart into exile...into the wilderness…only to leave me there. As the day came to an end I had two choices in front of me: turn once again to Scripture as I had each and every day for the past couple months, or go back to being content simply knowing about God, because I was obviously mistaken in how He communicates with us. Mercifully, I chose to talk. And to listen. And to expose my pouting soul and ask Him to console me. As I opened up the readings for the day, here is what I found.

> *For my thoughts are not your thoughts,*
> *neither are your ways my ways, declares the Lord.*
> *For as the heavens are higher than the earth*
> *so are my ways higher than your ways*
> *and my thoughts than your thoughts.*
>
> *For as the rain and the snow come down from heaven*
> *and do not return there but water the earth,*
> *making it bring forth and sprout,*
> *giving seed to the sower and bread to the eater,*
> ***so shall my word be that goes forth from my mouth;***
> ***it shall not return to me void,***
> ***but it shall accomplish the purpose for which I sent it.***
>
> *For you shall go out in joy*
> *and be led forth in peace;*
> *the mountains and the hills before you*
> *shall break forth into singing.*
> *And all the trees of the field shall clap their hands.*
> *Instead of the thorn shall come up the cypress;*
> *Instead of the brier shall come up the myrtle;*
> *and it shall make a name for the Lord,*
> *an everlasting sign that shall not be cut off.*
> *(Isaiah 55:8–13; emphasis added)*

As I put my defeated soul to bed that night, I managed to mutter, "Amen, Lord. I believe. I believe everything you have told me. I don't understand, but I believe. Please don't leave me."

CHAPTER 3

The Dance

The dance went on. We danced and we danced and I soon realized that I was falling in love with my God. So good He was to me! This new relationship kept me pining for that next opportunity to be still and really listen to Him. He continued to send His word to me daily. Such a faithful companion is He! And a good conversationalist too! The love notes and forget-me-nots were sprinkled throughout my days. Every now and then, He would send me a day when there was little in the way of communication. I still felt the connection to Him, but neither of us had much to say. On those days, I would stumble a bit. The accuser would sneak into the empty space and plant thoughts of "crazy" in my mind. "Surely, this whole conversation is a figment of your imagination," he would hiss. "Foolish girl, to think God is going to lead you home. There is nowhere for you to go! Tisdale has sold. Your desires are futile." But of course, satan is subtle, and so I had to hold captive every thought that entered my mind and examine it from all angles to determine from where it came. I would sit and examine, assess, and turn it on its head for perspective. Perhaps I *am* mistaken after all. I would try to generate some positive emotions concerning this exile my heart was in. I would continually proffer the suggestion that perhaps the Promised Land that I am waiting for is exactly where I am after all. Maybe a bit of gratitude will change my mind and bring me the peace that I am desperate for.

So I would sit and count my blessings. I would list all that I loved about the space I was living in so as to make sure that I was not deceiving myself. Occasionally, I would attempt to justify this longing to be somewhere else with thoughts of a reckless neighbor who abused those around him just as much as the alcohol he consumed. Or the vicious dog behind us that occasionally marked our territory as his own and sent my children scrambling up into the play set to avoid getting bit. These intrusions would enter my consciousness and create turmoil within my soul—a disquiet and agitation that I came to realize could not possibly be the voice of God. Yes, I felt called to a different place, but I needed to realize that this was ultimately a journey of my soul and really had nothing at all to do with my physical location. I never wanted this journey to be degraded to merely what makes me happy. This much I knew. I was completely and utterly incompetent to judge what would and would not make me happy. I was discerning enough to know that unless God built the house, I would forever remain unsettled.

The sole reason I hoped that a move would come to fruition was specifically because of my nomadic and restless heart. It was peace I was searching for. This much I understood. No matter where we ended up living, I was really seeking a place for my soul to put down roots and feel at rest rather than perpetually nomadic. That could happen where we currently lived or it could happen somewhere else, and so I made sure to keep all options on the table. "Lord, move us or give me peace." This was my mantra. So desperately I sought peace in my soul, but that goal proved to be elusive.

Looking back on my journey with God, it was always in thinking, calculating, and weighing that my soul was agitated. Tossing around pros and cons, practicing gratitude so as to change my frame of mind, trying to figure out where I was being led—all of this led to agitation. For sure, it all contributed to my understanding of God, but it is not where I found my peace. It is sometimes the case that in determining where God is not, we can discover where He actually is. My peace was found in the acceptance of His Word as manna for my soul that day. Looking back at Egypt did not bring me peace. Trying to figure out where my promised land was did not bring me peace. The peace came in simply enjoying and thanking God for the manna that came daily. So faithful He was! His mercies were new every morning. When I could take the little gifts as they came and simply thank God for them without trying to figure it all out, that is where I found my peace. My peace was in the minutes of the journey, not in the destination.

For a period of time, I was led to spiritual direction. These opportunities to meet with a faithful priest who could offer some insight into my soul was such a treat for me. Good fruit could always be found. Even if the gift wasn't immediate, I was always able to glean some good word of knowledge in the minutes and hours that followed these meetings. On one occasion, I met with a very kind elderly priest. The reputation of this ancient abbot as a spiritual director was quite favorable. My heart was overjoyed in anticipation of this privilege. I must have seemed quite naive and foolish that day as my thoughts spilled out of my mouth one after another in a rapid-fire succession.

This holy hero just smiled, held up one finger to silence me, and proceeded to hobble out of the room. I sat there, a bit stunned as I wasn't sure where he was going. After around ten seconds, he returned holding a little pamphlet. As he handed it to me, he simply mumbled, "Your mind is too busy. Read this."

And that was that! I was a bit astounded by the abrupt ending to my monologue, but I went ahead and walked outside eager to read whatever it was that God wanted to communicate to me in that publication. And good fruit there was! It was a pamphlet with Saint Mother Theresa on the cover. In bold print, were these two simple words: "I thirst."

Indeed, I do, I thought. But as I read it, I realized that it was God who was thirsting for *me!* This blew my mind. I knew He loved me. I knew He even died on the cross for me. But this was a message specifically for my heart that day. You see, I was very familiar with the feeling of *thirsting* for my God. This is exactly how I described my insatiable quest to know Him and to understand Him. It was a thirst that just could not be quenched. I would often stare at the plaque outside the Adoration Chapel at my parish. The words just found a home in my soul as I would contemplate my evolving relationship with God. "As a deer longs for springs of water, so my soul thirsts for you, O God" (Psalm 42:1). Yes, my soul was thirsting, and this thought was at the forefront of my mind as I went to my meeting that morning. So in this moment, to contemplate that God felt the same exact way about me was just amazing to me. In all my faults, failures, and floundering, still God thirsts for *me*! He does not simply tolerate me in my relentless and pitiful neediness, but rather He thirsts for little ol' me. Yes, this brief moment of spiritual direction placed a tremendous gift in my soul of knowing just how very much my God desires *me*. I understood that He enjoys our time spent together every bit as much as I do!

A bit further down the road, I began to meet with a different priest who was a bit better at conversation. At one of the appointments, Father recommended a series of books on discernment by Fr. Gallagher. These books took me deep into the spirituality of St. Ignatius and the rules to apply so as to understand the movements of my soul. Admittedly, upon reading his second book, I was taken a bit deeper into these exercises than I was designed for. The "math" became a bit too complicated for me. I began to compute what was from God, and what may have been the angel of light masquerading as God so as to deceive me. In this detour, my soul once again became agitated. I was doing too much calculating, too much head, and not enough heart. Knowing that satan would try to lead me astray by first appearing to be a good idea, how could I ever really be certain that *anything* was from God after all? I became confused.

This more complex discernment was troubling me, and so I realized that it was not where God wanted me to walk. I thanked St. Ignatius for his time as we parted ways. I was grateful for his contribution to my journey, and I learned some valuable lessons that I will forever keep with me. But my walk with him as a student came to an end as he introduced me to one of his good friends. It was at the feet of St. Therese that I learned how God wanted to commune with me. He walks a very unique journey with each and every one of us according to the way that He designed us. It was in this Little Flower that I found a kindred spirit. Peace was once again restored in reading *The Story of a Soul*, the autobiography of St. Therese of Lisieux. Her relationship with her God was so simple and pure and child-like. God spoke to her very quietly through His creation, and she just accepted it all as a lovely gift. Her spirituality was absolutely dripping with coincidences. Love notes from God sprinkled around her. In seeing a flower plucked out of the ground for her by her father, she noticed the delicate roots still attached to it, and in that flower, she saw herself. She realized that she was destined for a different soil. In that little flower, she saw the will of God that she would be transplanted. Only a soul deeply in love with God could be assured of the accuracy of that assessment. For the wayward child, that flower would likely remain only a flower and to claim that God's will could be summed up in such an inconsequential moment could prove to be foolish indeed if you are not accustomed to listening to His voice in the first place. On the contrary, the pilgrim who is earnestly seeking God in the moments of their day will discover Him again and again in the simplicity of everyday life. Little, seemingly inconsequential gifts that altogether make a tapestry unfolding before you pointing in the way you should go. To the soul that is seeking Him in the minutes of their day, who clearly recognizes His voice because they have "heard" it so often, these gifts of reassurance are great treasures.

In reading the words of St. Therese, I could see the littleness of myself. I, too, would encounter God in nature. He would give me many lovely gifts there, but in my calculating, I would brush them aside as nothing more than my foolishness looking too deeply into things. Reading *The Story of a Soul* gave me the freedom to simply accept these little gifts for what they were. God was indeed speaking to me in quiet little ways each and every day. And His still soft voice was especially deafening when outside in the stillness of nature. Yes, Ignatius had taken me as far as I was ready to go with him. His spirituality was too big for me. Too calculating. God was calling me to be little and just to accept His gifts as from the hand of a loving Father. I decided in that moment to accept them as they came without questioning from where they came. If it was a good and lovely thought, if it brought consolation to my soul, if it was not accusatory or belittling, then I accepted it. I gave satan no credit for any good thought that came my way. If he was going to attempt to deceive me, then so be it. I understood that God knows how vulnerable I am, how little I am, and he will protect me from any spiritual attack. Should I be led astray, my Shepherd would protect my heart and lead me back.

One morning, in particular, one of my readings was the story of Gideon who asked God for a clear sign so that he could rest assured that the hand of God was indeed in what he felt led to do. And a sign he received—not once but thrice! After reading this story, I sat there thinking about this road I was traveling. A year had passed by now since Tisdale had sold. A whole year! And I was still homesick. I was still longing for Tisdale. I was still asking God each and every day how He was going to make sense of all that stirred in my soul. I asked not to be moved. And I asked not to stay. All I knew was that I needed peace. I just really needed to know that it was truly God's will that I keep walking this road. Knowing how easily we can deceive ourselves, like Gideon, I too wanted a sign that would show me that the desire of my heart was indeed placed there by God and that I should continue to discern where my home was. "Just give me a sign that you are, in fact, leading me. Let me know that I am not foolishly deceiving myself. Show me that this desire is from your hand. You don't even have to tell me how the journey ends. Just give me a sign. Something tangible so that I can say, 'There you are!'"

A couple hours later, I went to my parents' house. *Coincidentally*, my brother stopped by briefly to shuffle kids around at the same time, and *coincidentally* he said, "I drove by your old house today!"

"You did!? Waterfall?" I asked. This seemed logical to me, as our Waterfall property was close by.

"No," he said. "Tisdale!" This house that we hadn't lived in for around eight years now. This house that was located at the end of a long private drive off of a side road that led to nowhere so that one would have to go completely out of their way in order to drive past it. This house that my brother had no idea that I was pining for. Yes, this is the house that he just so happened to drive by that day. He didn't just drive by the road that led to our road either. He went out of his way to make the trek down the long private drive that led to nowhere in order to see our old house. Did I mention that I had asked God for a sign? Well played, God. Well played.

I could write an entire book on all the gifts that have been given to me. All the love notes sent my way. But suffice it to say that my God drew me very deeply into communion with Himself.

> As the deer longs for streams of water, so my
> soul thirsts for you, O God. (Psalm 42:1–6)

Yes, I was longing, pining, thirsting for my God. I was insatiable. After some time, the desire for a specific place known as Tisdale dissipated. However, the nomadic homesick feeling remained, though I knew not for where. I longed to go home, but I could not tell you where "home" was. A square peg in a round hole is what I remained. After a while, I was led to spend time with Him frequently in Adoration, and then finally, I was led to daily Mass. I am not a morning person by nature, and yet I was naturally waking without an alarm early enough that I could attend the 8:00 a.m. Mass each day. At one point, a lovely parishioner approached me after Mass and said, "I just wanted to let you know that I have been praying for you and your family. I don't know why, but you have been on my mind and so I have been keeping you in prayer." I thought little of the remark other than to acknowledge the thoughtfulness of the gesture. I remember saying from time to time that there was a reason that God wanted me at daily Mass. For some reason, He planted the desire in my heart to meet Him daily, and then he changed my physiology for a time so that it was natural for me to awaken early enough to be with Him.

I had been dancing with my God for around three years at this point. The union was deep and unshakable. I had been holding onto him for so long that I wouldn't know how to let go. To go back to the anemic conversations that defined our relationship in the past was unthinkable. My God was molding and shaping my soul. He was teaching me to lean on Him. Little did I know that the greatest trial of my life was about to begin, and my good God was preparing my heart to trust Him.

CHAPTER 4

Surrender

While finishing up my shopping after Mass one morning, a text came through that was sent out to the entire family. It was Mom. "We just got the test results. It is cancer." We had been awaiting results concerning a suspected prostate cancer in my dad. I allowed those few words to sink in as I finished making my purchases. As my head was spinning, I ran into a most dear friend of our family. Surely, people must have thought I was crazy as my emotions escalated to the point of hysterics. She simply asked how I was doing, and that was all it took to open the floodgates.

"Cancer! He has cancer!" Tears were streaming down my cheeks as I choked on the words.

"It will be alright," Sandy reassured me as she wrapped me in an embrace. Trying to regain my composure, I simply nodded. "Really, it will," she continued. "Everything will be alright." That was good enough for me in that moment. This friend of ours is what is known as a living saint. If Sandy says everything is going to be okay, then it's going to be okay. My mom and I would joke about that from time to time whenever we felt overwhelmed. "No worries. Sandy said every-thing would be alright." While it was said tongue in cheek, it did, in fact, console us. This happenstance of running into her at that exact moment was as good as a message from God Himself letting us know not to worry. God does indeed use people to communicate with us, and this day, He used Sandy. Everything was going to be alright.

More tests would follow. Soon we would learn that not only did he have cancer, but there were two different types of cancer, and they were very aggressive. In my mind, I kept thinking that at some point, we would receive the silver lining that would put our fears to rest, and it did come in time, but at that moment, things continued from bad to worse. This was not the slow-growing, no-big-deal cancer that my grandpa had. This was bad, and we were waiting to hear just how bad.

I will forever remember this moment as a turning point in my life. One moment, life was blissful. Stressful on occasion and busier than I would have preferred, but blissful and carefree nonetheless. Everything was good in every sense of the word. Life was just *truly* good. Family gatherings were untarnished by the burden of tragedy. Daily life had a melody that was sweet and light. I knew that suffering existed, but until now, it couldn't touch us. But then, in the very next moment, everything was affected. Our family had been touched by the finger of tragedy and our illusion of safety disappeared.

Weeks passed by, and my dad's life was hanging in the balance as we waited with bated breath the results of his scans. They were looking to see if the cancer had spread to his other organs or bones. The next few hours would determine the fate of my father, and I was afraid. I went to Mass that morning to push my fears aside and allow God to comfort my soul. Instead of comfort, however, my spirit was blindsided by the readings that day. There I sat wondering if my dad was going to live and how strenuous was the path that lay before him. As my attention was drawn to the lector in front of me, the words came from 1 Peter 4:7–11.

> *The end of all things is near. Therefore, be alert and of sober mind so that you may pray. Above all, love each other deeply, because love covers over a multitude of sins.*

Oh, how I hoped my mom wasn't reading this verse on this day. It certainly did have an ominous feel to it. As Mass finished, I knelt down to plead with God. I begged for the life of my father. As I sat in turmoil, a curious conversation filled my thoughts.

"Would you take his place?"

The thought would not leave me. In my training the past few years, it has occurred to me that when a thought refuses to leave you alone, and there is peace in your soul, then you should entertain it. As I tossed it back and forth, this came out. "I wish I could say that I trust You enough to take his place. It's not for lack of love for him. Indeed, if it were only me, I should say take me instead. But I don't know how that would be any easier on the family! After all, I have children who need me. I'm sorry, but no matter how much I love him, and no matter how much I love You, for the sake of my family, I just can't say I would take his place." I realized there was a lack of trust in this response, but I trusted that God understood that it came from a place of love for my family. But there was a pushback, a follow-up question: "Would you allow one of your children to take his place?"

That one thought that drifted across the plain of my consciousness was startling to say the least. Just the thought of sacrificing one of my children to the will of God, not knowing what that might mean was enough to make my knees buckle! How in the world could I even entertain such a thought! Our entire existence is wrapped up in our beloved children! No. I absolutely could not do that. But then...

Thoughts of a conversation that I had with my sister not too long before came flooding back to me. We contemplated the sacrifice of Abraham. We struggled with what a difficult story that is. How could a good God ask such a thing of his friend? How can you reconcile this request with what we know about the nature of God as *love* personified? We touched on how it was a foreshadowing of the sacrifice of God's only Son. We discussed how he was holding it up in contrast to the human sacrifices that were common practice during that time. But still, we were disturbed by the thought. We can look at it from this side of history and conjecture the reasons why God made the request, and we can try to understand the significance of it. But we have to consider the reality that in that moment existed a real person who had to reconcile this very difficult request with the trust he had in his God.

As I sat in that quiet sanctuary, I was able to clearly see the thread of communication and revelation that began with this conversation concerning Abraham, and I could connect it with this new conversation that God was now initiating with me. In that moment, I came to realize that God asks for no less from each of us! We are all called to acknowledge that everything we have belongs ultimately to God, and that includes our families. These children are gifts, but they do not belong to us. My Father was asking me to loosen my grip and to entrust them to His care for better or worse. I can't say I had enough trust for such complete and reckless abandonment to the will of God. I only realized that this is what I was called to. Such a total act of surrender was beyond what I was capable of offering, even if it was to the Creator of the universe who loves my children more than I could possibly imagine!

After much reflection on the question before me and recognizing how the potential loss of one of my children would be far too much to bear, the best I could do was to offer the one we did not yet know—the one who we had not yet had the privilege of meeting in order to see his personality and to experience his thoughts, the one in whom we had not yet witnessed his sweet smile or his little voice. The most I could offer was this: "I offer my unborn baby. Taking one of my older children would be too much to bear for the entire family including me. We already know them through and through. I offer the baby in my womb because that would be primarily my cross alone. It would be painful for everyone, but they do not yet know him. But instinctively, biologically, and mystically, I know him. It would be my heartbreak. It would be the only thing that I could offer that would be a deep and painful sacrifice solely for me, thereby protecting, to some extent, the hearts of my family."

And the conversation was finished.

Immediately, my rational brain kicked in and tried to reassure me that certainly God would not ask such a thing of me. But still, against all reason, against all instincts, against the deep and abiding love for my unborn son that would protect him at all cost, I renewed my vow. Out of love for my God, trusting that He would never do anything to hurt me, knowing that He loves me and my baby desperately, I muttered a quick "I won't go back on my word. But please don't take him from me." Kind of a "let this cup pass…not my will, but thine" moment. I made the sign of the cross on my precious baby nestled within me as I stood up to leave. I was fully aware of the profound conversation that had just taken place but was unsure of whether or not it was truly God. Perhaps it was just my way of trying to "fix" something that was un-fixable. Either way, just the thought of losing my unborn baby should have been enough to incapacitate me—and yet amazingly, it was just as quickly forgotten as I went about my day.

Not more than thirty minutes later, we received word that this aggressive cancer had not spread to my dad's bones or organs. We were looking at surgery for sure, followed by hormone and radiation therapy, but no chemotherapy. This was good. This was our silver lining. His prognosis remained favorable, and so we buckled up to go through the paces with him.

This act of surrender that I made to my God was forgotten by me for the most part. It did not cause any turmoil in my soul amazingly enough. It wasn't until a couple weeks later that it returned to my attention, but not in the way I would have expected. In offering God admittance through that cracked door of surrender, a journey began that would demand much of me. This journey would call me to a tremendous sacrifice. But my unborn baby was not the sacrifice He was asking of me. He took the cross that I *offered* to carry and adjusted it a bit—custom crafted it for our family and asked something else of us entirely. He fashioned a cross that was heavy enough that our entire family would be brought to our knees in carrying it but not so heavy that it would crush us. It was sufficiently large that our family of eight children plus mom and dad could all carry it together. But at the center of the cross was not my unborn son. Instead God placed the one in our family whom He knew could withstand the brunt of the suffering and could do it beautifully and gracefully. At the center of this cross, He placed my beautiful eight-year-old boy, Sam.

CHAPTER 5

Shipwrecked

It was a Tuesday in June, and we were just about to settle into our evening. We had arrived home from a beach vacation with the cousins two days prior. We had wrapped up our second day of Vacation Bible School that morning. "Shipwrecked" was the theme, and "God saves!" was the message. I was in the kitchen preparing dinner, and Dave was relaxing on the front porch after arriving home from work a few minutes prior. Sam skipped into the kitchen, seeking a snack from the refrigerator. I cautioned him to close the door seeing as how we would be eating soon. He bounced back out of the room as if not a thing in the world were any different on this day. It couldn't have been more than a minute later when a cry came from around the corner in the living room. Through tears, Sam announced that he had a headache. The tears were very much out of character for him, and it seemed to set in so quickly that I was a bit alarmed. I immediately went for the Ibuprofen. I knew from experience that Tylenol never really seemed to help his headaches very much.

As I was on my way back to Sam, he began screaming and writhing in pain, grasping at his head. Trying not to panic, I hurried toward the porch to summon Dave, but he was already on his way inside upon hearing the screaming. It took all of five seconds to deduce that he needed medical attention, and so we put his shoes on him. Sam was crying, pleading with me, and asking if he was going to be okay.

"Yes, of course, sweetie. You're going to be okay. The medicine will kick in soon, and you'll be feeling better. We are just going to take you in to get checked out." All of this I was blurting out as Dave was leading him to the van. I didn't believe a word of it myself, but I tried my best to create the illusion of confidence. Halfway through the kitchen, Sam's legs went out from under him and just...stopped working. Dragging behind him, lifeless, for a moment before Dave swept him up in his arms. By the time we made it to the garage, which was a mere ten feet away, my Sam...my sweet, sweet Sam was unresponsive. *It was 5:10 p.m.*

Oh, how precious and terrifying and life-changing is this moment in time in my memory. If I could only go back and wrap my arms around that sweet baby and make it better. If only I could go back to that moment and console that grief-stricken mother and father and tell them it will be okay. This was our moment when everything in existence came to a screeching halt. The world in those next few moments stopped spinning on its axis. The defining moment when our ever-after became entirely different than our reality one-minute prior. The terror in my heart should have killed me, except by the grace of God.

"Call 911!" Dave shouted as he carried our son's lifeless body over to the couch. My eyes scanned the room but couldn't immediately land on my phone.

"Where's my phone?" I shrieked. Instantly, my gaze went to the counter and located my phone in the midst of the chaos of family life that was strewn about all over the surface. I was shaking from head to toe as my hands clumsily tapped those three digits. I don't think I have ever truly understood what it means to panic until that moment. It felt as if the blood in my veins stopped flowing. The words that escaped came out without the use of breath, as I had no breath in my body. I was shaking uncontrollably. And yet I continued to do what must be done for the sake of my child. I continued to have that conversation with the dispatcher. I choked out my address, unsure that they could understand my wavering words. I listened to make sure Sam was breathing. I tipped his chin back to open his airway. I kept yelling at him to try to help him maintain consciousness. I don't even remember if any tears were flowing. I don't think they were as every-thing in my body was completely arrested as I went into autopilot to protect my son. I don't remember who was around, where my other children were, or what Dave was even doing in those moments. All I remember is working through the panic. Looking at Sam and feeling as though I might die right there with him. Waiting for what seemed like an eternity for the paramedics to show up, though in reality it was only a couple minutes. I later learned that the kids were ushered downstairs by a friend who was visiting. Dave was flagging down the EMS to hurry them inside. I can't recall how many people were in our house working on Sam. Just the broken record of a thought in my head: *Please. Just get him to the hospital! This is taking too long... just get him to the hospital!*

The next thing I remember, I was in the front seat of the ambu-lance, staring out at the expanse of sky in front of me. Lights and sirens blaring, highways not an option due to construction, the eter-nal drive to the hospital as my son lay behind me. Occasionally I would force myself, despite my fear, to turn around and look at Sam. My search always proved futile, however, as my senses could perceive nothing of the reality of what was happening to my son. All I knew was that he was not awake. The hospital was notified that we were on our way. And the sirens were blaring, so it must be serious.

On wobbly legs, I hoisted my pregnant self out of the ambu-lance as I hurried to keep pace with Sam as he was wheeled into the hospital. Instantly, two advocates turned up on either side of me, standing close as I witnessed the mob of medical personnel descend on my son like a large screen showing of a suspenseful movie. The blue stage curtains perfectly framed the doorway so that I wouldn't miss a single moment of the drama unfolding before me. Visible to me were the bottoms of Sam's new tennis shoes as he lay lifeless and unsuspecting on the table, unaware of the large steel scissors cutting his clothing off of him. I was horrified. There he lay. Still. Cold. Naked. Oblivious to the poking, prodding, and jostling from all sides.

Good Lord, I thought. *He would be so mortified right now if he knew what was going on!*

"Do you want a wheelchair?" I was asked for the third time.

"No," I answered. "I am fine." If I sat down, if I allowed that bit of weakness to overtake me, the rest of me would collapse and not recover. Standing made me strong. As long as I was standing, I was okay. As long as I was standing, I was not beat.

Dave was standing, witnessing, processing all that was unfolding just the same as I was. He had arrived by car not long after us and slipped in to find his son lying there naked. This was the moment when he too realized just how critical of a situation we were in. It was explained to us that something was going on inside Sam's brain. He had been in a constant seizure since he presented, his pupils were both blown, and they were taking pictures to find out exactly what had transpired inside his beautiful head.

They wheeled my Sam back for a CT as they brought me his shoes in a plastic bag. Not more than a couple minutes later, a new face approached us—a face that would remain with us for the long haul. It was Sam's neurosurgeon, Dr. Chen. She explained that Sam had a large bleed on his brain, which she suspected was due to a tangle of blood vessels that had ruptured. As it turned out, she was spot on. It was indeed an Arteriovenous Malformation or AVM that had ruptured. In a demeanor that only a neurosurgeon can balance, with grace and gentleness mixed with cold, hard facts, she delivered the first punch. Sam had to go back for emergency brain surgery. There were many question marks in his future, including survival. At this point, we had to accept the possibility that he may not survive the surgery. If surgery was successful, the next five days would be critical as his brain continued to writhe and swell and ultimately die to some extent from the trauma that had been inflicted upon it. I looked at the shoes I was holding, and I couldn't help but wonder if he would be wearing them home or if they would become a monument to my dead son.

Oh my heart. Such a futile task to try to capture in words the emotion of a mother's heart that has been torn in two. It was night. Not an ordinary night. A deep, dark, bottomless, hopeless, terrifying, empty night—full to the brim with despair. My soul resisted going down into this darkness, but I realized that I had no choice. One foot and then the next and the next and the next like a lamb to the slaughter. My prayers were without words. I kept looking up from the bottom of this pit, but I was incapable of forming a coherent thought to call out to my Savior. I just asked that He take my tears, the groanings of my heart, and turn them into something beautiful because I was completely empty.

As Sam was rapidly wheeled past us, still lifeless on his bed, we followed behind. They were taking him to the OR for emergency life-saving surgery. I feebly requested that he be anointed by a priest before going back but was told that there wasn't time. My shaking hands again did what they needed to do as they grappled inside my purse and pulled out a bottle of holy water from Lourdes. My trembling thumb traced an old rugged cross on the forehead of my son. He looked so incredibly beautiful and precious to me. He was completely unaware of the devastation occurring inside his sweet head at that moment. There was no pain, no grimace. His eyes were closed as if in a peaceful sleep. One of the doctors started to engage in conversation with me but stopped short and simply said, "We've got to go." They ripped him away from me as one of the advocates asked if I wanted to give him a kiss goodbye. The team wheeling him away hesitated to see if I needed to catch up for a kiss. I declined. This wasn't goodbye, and I didn't want to hold them up from the work that needed to happen. I waved them forward and blew him a "see you later" kiss.

Certain scenes from our journey come to mind like snapshots that altogether create a story. His desperate cry, "Mom, am I going to be okay?" His naked body, lifeless and unsuspecting. His empty shoes in my hand, detached from his body. And now covered with a sheet, my baby who appeared to be doing nothing more than taking a nap was being wheeled away from me down the long cold hall as concerned eyes betrayed the team who was trying to console me.

There we stood, just the two of us with our advocates. Both of us were too broken to be of any use to the other. In movies, and I suspect in real life on some occasions, as couples receive a devastating blow or enter into a crisis situation, they collapse in each other's arms and there are tears and hugs and support. We were none of those things to one another. We were empty vessels, unmoving, staring out into an unknown future with vacant eyes. We had nothing to offer the other. All we could do was wait as the minutes ticked by, as my son lay open on an operating table, as his life and our life as we knew it hung in the balance.

As we sat in darkness, a thought occurred to me. And then it occurred to me again. And then again. This familiar pattern caused me to take notice. It was a comforting thought. It was an enlightening thought. It was a tiny thought that was laced with hope. A tiny spark darting amidst the rubble.

This could have...no should have...taken place another way. At another time. There are a million reasons why this should have happened at a time when we wouldn't be able to respond as quickly as we did. It should have happened a few days ago when we were playing in the ocean. It should have happened in the mountains as we were driving home with no reputable hospital nearby. It should have happened while Sam was outside playing by himself on our property out of earshot of any of us. It should have happened when the kids were home alone, and I was out getting groceries or at the very least when Dave was still at work. But it didn't. It happened just after we arrived home from vacation and just after Dave arrived home from work. And right in front of us so that we could see him the very moment he went down and get help right away.

Divine providence was not lost on me. I recognized this voice. This was the voice of my God. He was reaching into my darkness, into this pit, and asking me to take His hand. This glimmer of hope did not make everything better. It did not fix *anything*. But it was a thought that gave me just enough to survive. It was manna. If I looked back, I crumbled. If my mind contemplated the "what ifs" of the future, I nearly fell off the precipice I was clinging to. But if I simply accepted that manna, that small thought of hope, that gift of consolation in the idea that God had it under control, then I could survive the moment. I could breathe my next breath. I could take the next step that I needed to take.

This good thought from my God would be affirmed again and again in various ways as we journeyed further down this path. But in that moment, that was enough. My God had trained me well to hear His voice over the past few years and so I could recognize Him. I could trust Him. Trust doesn't mean that you are not afraid. It doesn't mean that you aren't in a dark place. It simply means that you make a choice to turn towards Him in the midst of all of that. I was terrified. I was devastated. But I chose God in the midst of that darkness. I chose to put it in His hands, to acknowledge that it already was in His hands. I united myself with the Blessed Mother at the foot of the cross as I truly was on Calvary with her. Sam was on the cross with our Lord as Mary and I cried tears for both of them. Looking at her Son's crucified body and trying to process everything that was happening, still she trusted knowing that this was all within God's plan. The agonizing pain remained as she embraced His divine plan. Choosing not to despair does not make it hurt any less. Crosses are painful, but they can be carried with such grace, and we have our Blessed Mother as a beautiful example of how to suffer well, to remain at the foot of the cross even as we are suffering.

After a few hours, Sam came out of surgery. He survived.

I wish I could say that we heaved a sigh of relief, but we had to immediately steel ourselves for phase 2. The next five days would be critical. He would be fighting for his very life in the PICU as his brain continued to swell and die to some extent before he could begin the work of healing. It was impossible to know at that point exactly how much damage had been done. We would have to wait for the dust to settle before we could scan his brain again to find out exactly the extent of the damage. For now, he was critical but stable, and Dr. Chen needed to prepare us for what we were about to see when we went back to be with our son.

She explained that she had to remove a large portion of his skull to allow his brain to swell. His head would be shaven. He would have staples clear around in the form of baseball stitches. These staples would begin at his hairline in the middle of his forehead and run clear to the back of his head before wrapping around and ending at his sideburn by his right ear. He would have electrodes connected all over the top of his head with wires running off them. He would be on a ventilator, and so we would see a large tube coming out of his mouth. He would also have another small tube going in through his nostril.

We would see more lines and IVs entering his body at various ports, a catheter, EKG leads, and a tube inserted into his head to allow drainage. She explained how his head, where the bone was missing, could swell quite a bit—to the point where it would look quite grotesque.

I did not care. I truly didn't. In hindsight, the image is anxiety provoking. But in that moment, I just needed to see my son! I needed to hold him to whatever extent I could, which, as it turned out, was nothing at all. I was desperate to console him, to let him know that I was there with him. I didn't know what he would be aware of, but I needed to be with my son. My heart did not care that it would be bothered by all the lashings he took on Calvary. I just needed to run to him and hold him. It was every bit as awful as she prepared us for. He looked like hell. And yet, he looked beautiful at the same time. My sweet, sweet sleeping Sam.

As the evening progressed, I began to think obsessively about his last sentence, "Am I going to be okay?"

I lied to him.

I told him he was going to be okay.

He is most certainly not okay.

My mother's heart winced in pain at the promise that I made him. It bothered me in the very depths of my being that I could not make good on that promise. I could not make it okay. It is the most helpless feeling in the world to be unable to fix something of this magnitude for your child. I promised him he would be fine, and my heart was in pieces to know that I couldn't do a damn thing for him.

But here's the thing about rock bottom; the thing about being completely helpless is that your only recourse is to God. You've got nowhere else to go! Oh, you could stay in your desperation and darkness. But if you truly want to climb out of that pit, the only place you can possibly turn is to your God. The doctors had done all they could do. All that was left was to place him in the hands of Jesus to pray and to wait.

A number of family and friends had joined us throughout the course of the evening. Because I hadn't time to have Sam anointed before the surgery, Fr. Bearer would administer this sacrament as he waited in recovery. He brought with him a couple of people from his healing ministry, Peter's Shadow—Mary Beth, whom I had known for years, and Mike, a new face to me. As they stood by Sam's bedside, their voices began to swell in a gentle melody.

I will come to you in the silence.
I will lift you from all your fear.
You will hear my voice
I claim you as my choice
Be still and know I am here.

I am hope for all who are hopeless
I am eyes for all who long to see.
In the shadows of the night
I will be your light.
Come and rest in me.

Do not be afraid I am with you.
I have called you each by name.
Come and follow me, I will bring you home.
I love you and you are mine.

I am strength for all the despairing.
Healing for the ones who dwell in shame.
All the blind will see.
The lame will all run free.
And all will know my name.

Do not be afraid I am with you.
I have called you each by name.
Come and follow me, I will bring you home.
I love you and you are mine.

I am the Word that leads all to freedom
I am the peace the world cannot give
I will call your name, embracing all your pain
Stand up, now, walk, and live

Do not be afraid, I am with you
I have called you each by name
Come and follow Me
I will bring you home
I love you and you are mine.

I was a puddle on the floor at these words. This song! This song was my song! This song haunted me literally each and every day for the past few *years*. It was my song to console my nomadic spirit during my journey with God all this time. As I sat in prayer at night, it was this song that would waft through my consciousness consoling my aching homesick heart. As I would drive home from Adoration, this song would be my companion. This song…*this* song that they chose out of nowhere was completely inspired. These were God's words to my heart this night. This was the second time that God spoke to me in a very profound way in the middle of our deepest pain.

As they wheeled Sam into his new home in the PICU, we were greeted by Anna, his nurse. She had just finished tucking Sam into his new home for the night. She was meticulous to make sure he had all he needed in that moment and then she turned to Dave and me. "Is there anything I can do for you guys?"

Tears welled up in my eyes as I desperately choked out, "I need something that you can't give me. I need you to tell me that he is going to be okay."

Anna very slowly, methodically, hesitantly said, "I…feel… like…he's going to be okay." I came to learn that this was certainly the Holy Spirit speaking through her as she later confided to me that she never gives parents false hope because she doesn't know that they *will* be okay. And so she never says so. But for some reason, in Sam's case, she truly felt that he would be okay, and against her better judgment, she felt compelled to speak those words to me. This was God-speak for the third time that night. I needed to be able to tell Sam that he would "be okay," as it bothered me so deeply that I promised him those very words. The Holy Spirit, through Anna—our modern-day prophetess—reassured me that we could make good on this promise. Indeed, Sam *would* be okay.

CHAPTER 6

In the Shadow of Death

Beep. Beep. Beep. Beep. Beep… steady as a metronome, the machines connected to my son were a constant and faithful reminder of the reality of what we were living through. Second by second, minute by minute, time crawled by as we watched with rapt attention the numbers on his monitor—heart rate, blood pressure, breaths per minute, and, most consequential, his ICPs, aka brain pressure. As long as his brain pressure did not creep up over twenty, then all was well—or so we were told. A gift we received early on happened immediately following his surgery. During those first few hours in the PICU, much to everyone's astonishment, Sam's ICPs remained in the negatives! I believe this promising beginning was the source of our wiggle room as the numbers would fluctuate in the days that followed. At times, the number would creep up close to and in some cases over that ominous 20 mark, but because the number started so low, it had room to climb as his brain protested in anger at the assault inflicted upon it.

When Anna checked his eyes on that very first night, she said nothing to us but called a second nurse in to look. Second opinions are anxiety provoking, and so we waited patiently to understand what the fuss was about. The second nurse confirmed Anna's assessment, and only then did she share with us that his pupils were "equal, reactive, and brisk." A good sign indeed, and so we joined in celebrating this minor victory. "Equal… Reactive… Brisk." This description

45

reverberated around the walls of his room each hour as they peeled back his eyelids to shine a flashlight in his vacant eyes.

As Sam lay there for days on end in what seemed to be an eternal slumber, I desperately longed to climb into his hospital bed, to hold him in my arms, to stroke his face and tell him that I was there, that everything would be okay. All of my mothering instincts were stifled, however, as my love was a deadly weapon to my son. The moment I touched my baby, his numbers protested angrily in response. I wouldn't even dream of rubbing his skin. Simply resting my hand on his arm was enough to place Sam in danger. His heart rate, blood pressure, and brain pressure all served to demonstrate just how desperately he hated touch. "Let him know that you are there! It's so important that he knows you are with him." And yet trying to console him only placed him in perilous territory, medically speaking. Wound care could not happen in those first few days. At least not without having medication ready to bring him back down. Sam's head and body continuously gravitated to a spastic fetal position as he slept with his chin resting on his chest. Hour by hour, we battled to keep his body straight so that he could breathe easier. Each time he was touched to adjust his position, to change his diaper, or to clean his wound, his body became stiff as a board as his ICPs flirted with that ominous 20 mark. Mostly, I just sat by his bedside looking at him, looking at his monitor, speaking softly, praying gently, rosary beads held tightly in my clenched fist. I perpetually teetered on the edge of blind faith and boundless hysterics. The lights remained dim so as to allow his brain time to heal with the least amount of aggravation. *Beep. Beep. Beep. Beep*…on and on it went, minute by grueling minute, every second lasting an eternity.

Each morning and each evening, Sam's team of professionals gathered outside the door of his room for rounds. It was truly mind-blowing to observe the tweaks and adjustments that were necessary to keep Sam alive. Around ten experts, doctors, nurses, nutritionists, pharmacy—all bouncing numbers and ideas off one another to find the perfect cocktail of interventions to keep him alive. The balance of the sodium in his body. The affects the different medications were having on him. This one caused his blood pressure to drop too low. That one caused his heart rate to elevate. What was his urine output? What was the weight of his soiled diapers? How much fluid was his drain collecting? How many neuro-storms was he having? Were they likely to be seizures? How well were we controlling his temperature fluctuations? Apparently injured brains need cool temperatures. His room was like an ice box. Regulation of his body temperature proved to be an elusive goal. A downward trend continued downward without intervention, and an upward trend continued upward. His clothing and blankets were stripped as he was placed on a cooling pad. His fever would drop as I watched my poor, naked, eight-year-old boy lying in this sterile hospital room unable to tell us if he was uncomfortable or in pain or scared. There Sam lay, dressed only in a diaper as I was bundled in multiple layers to remain comfortable. My mother's heart longed to wrap him in a blanket and make him warm, but such drastic measures were absolutely necessary to keep his temperature down. While meticulously watching his numbers to keep him cool, he absolutely could not shiver without risking injury. And so, upon successfully lowering his temperature to the point of shivering, they would instantly change directions and begin to warm him just a bit to prevent him from shaking. Adding only a light sheet caused his temperature to climb once again in an uninhibited trajectory until they intervened once again with an about-face. And so this dance continued until his brain learned how to regulate his body temperature once again. And so it went. Minute by minute changes to the cocktail of medications. Constant adjustments to keep his body straight in bed and medication to help him recover from being fussed with. Daily x-rays confirming that pneumonia was not setting in. Unsuccessful attempts at placing a soft boot on his foot to prevent foot drop. Respiratory therapists shaking him with a vest every four hours in order to prevent pneumonia. EKG leads removed and then added again as they suspected seizures. Removed a second time, and then placed once again. In the end, he was not having seizures. He was neuro-storming. These storms brewed up quickly and frequently and were quite difficult to watch. As his brain short-circuited, his heart rate jumped drastically up and down in a matter of seconds. His poor little body became one big spasm as he convulsed in his bed. His heart rate and blood pressure climbed dangerously high, but our eyes would always be on that one critical number—His ICPs (intracranial pressure). Realizing that any storm could further damage his brain, we held our breath as his ICPs crept close to and occasionally over twenty. He would typically hover between sixteen and twenty-three before coming back down. Rigor mortis would set in within our own bodies as we braced ourselves until the storm subsided. When Sam's muscles relaxed, ours did as well. Appropriately, the Mass readings during this time period often revolved around Jesus calming storms which brought a certain peace to my heart—mostly after the storm had passed.

Sam was on Fentanyl, Valium, and other life-saving medications. The one that was his saving grace was Versed. For a while, they gave Sam a Versed bolus each time a storm brewed up, but they soon discovered that he needed a continuous Versed drip in order to proactively minimize their frequency and severity. One night in particular, Sam began to storm once again. Nights were always worse. The storms came faster and were fiercer in the evenings and throughout the night. This one particular night, a violent storm descended on my sweet boy. His muscles contracted; *my* muscles contracted. His breathing and heart rate become erratic as did mine as I watched him. His intracranial pressure numbers began climbing and climbing as the storm refused to loosen its grip on my boy. Sending out a request for prayers, I sat beside Sam in the dark with my rosary in hand. I united myself with Jesus as I walked through the Sorrowful Mysteries of the Rosary at the bedside of my son. I couldn't help him. I couldn't console him. I had no idea if he even knew that I was with him. But I could pray, and so that is what I did.

As the beads rolled between my fingers, texts came through one right after another. Praying! *Ding!* Lifting you up in prayer! *Ding!* Offering a rosary now! *Ding!* Love you guys! *Ding!* I didn't even read them until later. I just knew that we were being lifted up, supported, embraced while we held Sam up to God. Bead after bead after bead, Sam continued to fight the swells that battered his already poor, ravaged body. At the end of the last decade of my rosary, all of Sam's numbers began dropping like a beautiful decrescendo until they leveled out and returned to normal by the time I uttered "Amen." It was the most profoundly beautiful prayer that I have ever experienced. Truly God was in that room with us—and our Blessed Mother as well. Their presence was palpable.

Sundays were often good days for Sam. One Sunday early on, as Sam was still on his ventilator enduring his own passion, God arranged for a steady stream of visitors to bless and anoint him. Even the nurses commented on "what a blessed little guy he is today!" He was absolutely bathed in grace from sunrise to day's end. Our own beloved Fr. Dave prayed for Sam during all masses that morning before coming to visit and pray over him. He always saved his daily rosary for the bedside of Sam. Additionally, Fr. Bearer brought the Mass to Sam right in his hospital room on this day! Arriving with his healing ministry team, he donned his vestments and proceeded to consecrate the bread and wine into Jesus's Body and Blood right there in that humble, sterile space.

As I gazed upon Sam with his staples, his ventilator, his eyes closed in the deep sleep of one on the brink of death, I was aware of his union with Christ. One passion. One cross. One suffering. They were united as Christ's Passion, Death, and Resurrection were made present once again right before our eyes. My focus would not remain on the death of Christ. I knew that a resurrection followed, and I began to hope that this would be Sam's destiny. He would be resurrected from this "death." One can never be entirely certain until it happens, but in that moment, my heart was able to finally embrace the idea that we would come out on the other side of this ordeal. We would be witnesses to His Resurrection in our son. Sam was anointed and blessed and prayed over all day long on this Sunday. Literally, from morning until evening, a constant stream of priests, deacons, and lay ministers were in and out of the room laying hands on Sam, speaking words of healing to him, anointing him with oil, blessing him with holy water, and announcing *life* to Sam's body and to our spirits.

Despite the tremendous gifts of consolation sent my way, I can't really express the pain and suffering in my heart. Any attempt at doing so would be sorely inadequate. My heart suffered for my son.

I suffered because I could not console Sam in any meaningful way. I could not hold him. I could not cuddle him. I couldn't even *touch* him. I didn't know if he was aware of anything, if he was afraid. Did he even know that I was with him? Did he know that I wouldn't think of leaving his side? Even if he was aware of my presence, would he remember me? Would he know who I am? Such a tremendous cross to not be able to kiss your child's boo-boo to make it better. Such a burden to watch your child suffer but to do nothing more than stand by helplessly.

Additionally, my heart ached for my children at home. I was too distracted, too far from them to understand how their hearts were processing all of this. The detachment that I felt from my children and husband was painfully bitter as well. I wanted to spend my days holding each one of my children to make sure they were okay, but my heart could not detach from the one who was in critical condition.

The roots of this ache reached out to my husband as well. He has always been so good at fixing problems. Anything I have ever needed, any problem I have ever experienced, Dave was always so terrific at getting to work nearly immediately to make sure it was taken care of. My heart ached for his heart. Just as I longed to do what I was designed to do—to hold and nurture, and care for Sam—Dave was longing to do the impossible as well. He was designed to protect him. He needed to fix the problem and make it go away. We were both so incredibly frustrated in our helplessness, and his heartache compounded my heartache.

My heart ached for our parents. Particularly my mom because as a mom myself, I know her heart. Not only could she not help Sam, but she could not help me. I imagined the double suffering of watching your child suffer for their child. Additionally, my dad was getting ready to endure his own passion as he went under the knife to rid his body of cancer, and I knew the brunt of that turmoil landed on my mom's poor heart. My heart ached for my unborn baby who would be making his entrance into the world in the midst of this mess. I ached as I considered my elevated cortisol levels and how that might affect my little one nestled within me. My. Heart. Ached. It was a deep, unreachable ache—a profound ache for Dave, for Charles, for

Amelia, for Sarah, for Claire, for Julianne, for Michael, for my baby, and, of course, for sweet, sleeping Sam—bearing the brunt of the cross on his shoulders, lying in bed for weeks on end as we awaited the day when he would wake up and come back to us.

Additionally, from our vantage point in the PICU, we were very much walking in the shadow of death. Death and suffering, heartache and pain absolutely engulfed us independent of what we were enduring, hanging thick in the air and dripping down the walls. It was impossible to escape. The weight of our environment added a darkness to our senses that was difficult to rise above.

God was faithful to us during the entire journey. Dave had his own "Morgan Freeman" moments when someone would pop up out of nowhere and encourage him, "Chin up. Everything's going to be alright." When Dave was at his lowest, he received what he needed to sustain him. From my perspective, the spiritual gifts were countless because I paid close attention. I waited for that next gift to sustain me. So very many coincidences could be found. Readings from Scripture that spoke to my heart. Experiencing the hands and feet and heart of Christ through family and friends around us as they took care of us and gave so sacrificially of themselves. I promise you; God painted the sky in Akron just for little ol' me. From the day we set foot in the PICU until the day we went home seventy-three days later, the sky followed my emotions. When I was sad, the sky was sad. When I was uplifted, so was the sky. When I felt confused and agitated, the rolling, turbulent, confused clouds felt the same way. When I was happy/sad, there would be curious raindrops on my windshield while the most beautiful sky was above me. Rainbows, rainbows, and more rainbows all about. I was well saturated with pictures friends had taken of a rainbow or two that came into existence as they were praying for Sam. One friend in particular mentioned multiple rainbows all about her during the hour that Sam entered his passion. Rainbows are a sign of hope, and they promised me good things in our future. Multiple days in a row, as I was traveling to and from the hospital, God painted the most amazing spectacle in the sky. Often it would be an awe-inspiring, jaw-dropping sunset, or simply amazing and colorful cloud formations. These skies were so captivating that people would physically stop on the side of the road and exit their cars so as to capture pictures of these amazing paintings in the sky. I suppressed the desire to stop and point out that those clouds were a gift for me! I don't suppose anyone would have taken me seriously.

After some time had passed, these formations set up camp in my rearview mirror each time I found myself in my car. When things pester me or repeat themselves, I have learned to take notice. After multiple breathtaking views set up camp behind me, I asked God, "Why are they always behind me right now? I want to see them! And you keep putting them in my rear-view mirror!" The thought wasn't even in my head more than a few seconds when my little four-year-old prophetess in the backseat spoke up.

Without even a hunch as to the thought in my mind, Julianne asked, "Did you know God is behind you?"

Surprised, I answered, "He is?"

"Yes," Julianne said. "He is whispering in your ear."

Surprising? Yes, of course. But then again, His gifts were coming daily and so I just added it to the pile.

Sam survived the first five critical days. As we crawled out of that dark cavernous pit and assessed the damage, it felt as if we had spent an eternity in the abyss facing the shadow of death. It was difficult to adjust to the light of expectation. Difficult to trust it. Barring any complications, it looked like we could rest in the hope that he would live indeed. He was still unresponsive but reacting to stimuli. His storms were under control for the most part. They were far fewer and easier to control. It was time to rescan Sam's brain to see where the dust had settled. The aftermath of a brain injury can be far more devastating than the actual injury itself.

At the time of the rupture, Dr. Chen could not tell us how much damage had been done other than to say he had a large bleed. Knowing that the brain would continue to die over the next few days, we could do nothing other than keep him stable and wait to see the wake of devastation left in the path of his rupture. As they wheeled Sam down the hall, I was just so thrilled that we had made it to this moment and that Sam seemed to be improving. I don't think

I fully comprehended how life altering his injury would be. We were about to come to terms with what our foreseeable future held. We were about to learn that the boy we came in with would not be the boy we brought home.

CHAPTER 7

The Beginning of Grief

Dr. Chen meandered into the room with Sam's CT results. "Well… I've seen worse," she said. Not comforting words to say the least. She presented us pictures of Sam's once perfect brain, now a mottled mess. On the left exists beautiful shades of gray, perfect fingerprints of his Creator. On the right side, darkness. Clots. Holes. An entire half of his skull, missing. It appeared as if the right hemisphere was completely stroked out. Gray shades were missing entirely as darkness enveloped what was once full of life only days before. I felt my body collapsing into the chair beneath me as she listed all the deficits he would suffer from. He would not come out on the other side the same boy we saw only a few days ago. Sam as we knew him would be a different person. He would be scarred with the lifelong deficits of someone with a neurological injury. He would suffer from left side deficiencies. His left hand "may" become a helper hand at best but would never function as before. He would have difficulty walking due to deficits in his left leg. He would never run again. His sense of smell would likely be affected. His personality would be markedly different. We would notice deficits with his processing speed, his logic and reasoning, cognitive abilities, executive function, and memory. He would need a brace to walk. Most things that he once enjoyed doing would no longer be possible. Thrill rides at Cedar Point would not likely be in his future. Ice skating and skiing, not possible. At least not possible as we had known it before. We were prepped on the world of "adaptive" everything. Adaptations for the home, adaptive sports, accommodations for his limitations.

I was devastated. I often wondered if I would have felt the same grief if Sam had grown up with these limitations. If I had never known him as he was. If I had never seen him run barefoot or climb, skip, or jump. If I had never enjoyed his quick wit or fun personality. If I had never enjoyed the things I was now going to miss, would I have grieved the loss of him in the same way? This grief was such an incredibly complicated emotion. I was grieving the loss of someone who was right in front of me. Grieving the playfulness that went away. Grieving the personality that would now be different. Grieving the loss of my son, really. But yet, my son was still with me. Although he would look a bit different than my son and act a bit different than my son, and move differently than my son, he is still my son! And still very much alive! How can you grieve the loss of someone while remaining grateful that they are still with you? Additionally, there was also the hope that some of "Sam" would be preserved. Some of who he was could be restored. And so it was difficult to grieve these things as something lost for good. While in the deep and painful throws of grief, my heart was telling me to hold onto hope! Don't give up! Don't settle there! Hold out for more restoration! My God was telling me that Sam would come back to us.

In an attempt to offer consolation, others would reach out to me with stories of how they found joy in the midst of their crosses. Many stories would cross my path of people who were thriving with their deficits—heroic stories of victories in the Paralympics, relationships that were better than ever despite the limitations of their loved ones. Countless occasions when the phrase "new normal" was lobbed my direction in an effort to help my heart heal. My heart just could not bear the thought of a "new" normal. I was pining for our old normal. Needing to adjust to a new normal was a lashing each and every time I contemplated it. I just wanted to go back to the way life was a few days prior. Looking at pictures of my Sam, I just couldn't bear to contemplate any kind of reality involving adaptations or labels or even the idea of a normal that involved Sam in a state that was even remotely different than before. The pain was not due to any sort of lamentation of having a disabled son, it was merely due to having a less-than-Sam Sam. My heart simply could not immerse itself in acceptance of a "new" normal. A "new" person. A "new" relationship. A "new" Sam. I was quite fond of the old Sam. Encouraging me to embrace the new was really a veiled attempt at asking me to detach from the old. Embracing one meant letting go of the other, and my heart could not be consoled in that thought.

In time, we began to shift our focus to the blessings of the prognosis. Silver linings were definitely evident if we chose to find them. Seeing as how the entire right hemisphere appeared completely stroked out, there was a surprising amount of blood flow to the outer peripheries of the brain. This would be inconsistent with completely stroked out tissue, and so there was some kind of life that we were not seeing, most likely masked by the residual swelling. Additionally, the midline of the brain did not shift more than a hair. For the first time, we were made aware of how incredibly blessed Sam was. "Even five more minutes. We would be having a very different conversation." Those were the words of Dr. Chen. I recalled my first glimpse of providence while Sam was in surgery. I remembered how God had pointed out His provision in allowing us to see and respond immediately when Sam suffered his hemorrhage. Yes, he would suffer painful changes and deficits, but the alternative of waiting even five more minutes and suffering a far worse fate—well, that was enough to drive us to our knees in thanksgiving.

We were pleased to learn that with more deliberate and purposeful parenting, Sam would continue to mature and grow up. We could expect him to find his way in the world in some manner. Perhaps not higher academic education, but he would be able to function to some degree in the adult world. He would remember us. He would remember everything, except perhaps a period of time, days to weeks, leading up to the stroke. While he would likely not be able to run or skip or hop or climb, we could at least expect that he would be able to walk, albeit with a brace and a compromised gait. Dr. Chen was fairly confident that he would be able to breath on his own and that he would likely be able to talk but that we may need to prepare ourselves for a more limited vocabulary and a slower processing speed.

Most of what we were saying goodbye to was life as we knew it, play as we knew it, personality as we knew it. In hindsight, it makes me chuckle to think of the very pointed questions we were asking Sam's doctor. In the grand scheme of things, that we should ask if he would be able to ride rollercoasters. She patiently answered our very ignorant and naive questions about thrill rides and wisely ignored the more obvious aspects of our struggles. Knowing our hearts could only handle so much devastation at a time, there was a great deal of information she kept from us.

What Dr. Chen did not tell us was that we were in it for the long haul. We could say goodbye to any semblance of normalcy for years. We were asking about rollercoasters, but our reality would involve far more consequential issues than rides at an amusement park! Learning to breathe again. Learning to talk again. Learning to eat again and swallow fluids. Months spent learning to use the bathroom independently again. Regaining strength to have enough head and body control for a ride in a car. His first couple months would be spent with no head control in a full-body wheelchair followed by a couple more months in a normal wheelchair. Our foreseeable future would involve six months of full-time daily therapy at the hospital followed by two months outpatient only to be discharged due to his plateau leaving little hope for more healing. Weeks spent in and out of the bathroom, mostly unsuccessfully, as our entire day would revolve around attempts to graduate from diapers. Upon graduation, a urinal would remain with us at all times due to a spastic bladder with zero patience for waiting even minutes for a bathroom. We were looking at a second surgery to replace his skull. A third surgery to remove it once again only to replace it with a plastic plate. Taking him through the very flat personality of a brain injury and fighting to recover some form of his personality. A spastic foot that would roll on itself, making barefoot walking impossible and uneven ground such as sand his nemesis. Bikes and swing sets, running, hopping, skipping, jumping, imagination, and play were all the things we would need to grieve the loss of. And here we were asking if he would ever be able to ride on a rollercoaster again. We had no idea that our son would remain so hindered by his body that his left side would be useless to him—that he would, without years of therapy, hobble around the house in the body of an old man constantly injuring himself as gravity became a cruel tyrant, throwing him violently to the ground whenever he tried to stand up or walk. We had no idea as to the gravity of what we were dealing with, and Dr. Chen wisely gave us only the information that was necessary in that moment and only answered our questions with simple answers shielding us from the questions we were not asking.

Despite the black-and-white prognosis, signs of hope could even be found in the words of the medical professionals. Dr. Chen consoled us with the assurance that she always prays before every surgery. Nurses expressed how it was the miracles that got them through the tough times. Seeing the impossible becoming possible from time to time sustained them in order to continue the work of caring for the critically ill and injured. In a conversation with Sam's neurologist, we asked if there might be any reason to hope for more. Her kind eyes smiled at us as she offered a bit of encouragement. "There is *always* reason to hope." Yes, God was weaving messages of hope to us through the words of those caring for Sam. God was, indeed, in that hospital, and His Spirit permeated the souls of those doing His work.

CHAPTER 8

Turbulent Waters

After some time, the team agreed that it was necessary to take Sam off the sedating drugs in order to attempt to extubate. Their plan of action was to wean his medications throughout the night, finally omitting his 8:00 a.m. meds altogether and then attempt to extubate sometime that morning or afternoon. Cutting medications cold turkey seemed risky to me. Oh, how we loved our Versed drip! It kept us nice and happy. Trusting the advice of the professionals, however, we braced ourselves for the turbulent waters that awaited us the next day.

Sam's last dose of medication was given sometime in the wee hours of the morning. As the drugs left his body, he remained pretty calm all night. My spirit slumped a bit as the sun rose in the sky that morning revealing nothing but gray as far as the eye could see. A relentless, cold, dreary drizzle presented itself announcing that it was likely to hang around awhile. Soon after sunrise, the first neuro-storm developed. It was a mini storm, but it served as a warning that without medication, Sam would remain vulnerable to more of the same. We were warned that they wanted to "see what he would do on his own" without medication. They planned to allow him to storm for fifteen minutes before coming to his rescue with Versed to see if he could calm the storm without medical intervention. The idea was incredibly unsettling as we knew that any storm could further damage his brain. We had spent the last week and a half working to avoid neuro-storms at all costs, and now we steeled ourselves to allow it to grip our child.

Not much more than thirty minutes after this first mini storm came a second wave that was fierce and terrifying. The only people around to witness this spectacle were Dave, myself, and Sam's nurse. The storm increased very quickly in severity. Sam's poor body went rigid. His arms and legs outstretched and shaking. His face flushed. His blood pressure climbed as his heart rate soared well above 200 bpm. Sam was hyperventilating and shook the bed with each breath. His nurse contacted *someone* by phone to keep them updated on how he was tolerating this storm. Terrified by what we were witnessing, we stood helplessly at the foot of his bed, praying for Jesus to calm the storm once again. Upon hanging up the phone, we were told that they wanted to allow him continue for a few more minutes. We watched as his chest heaved up and down in distress while his numbers climbed up, up, up!

In hindsight, I want to yell at them to "Stop! Give him the medicine! This is not working!" But in the moment, I just chose to trust the "person behind the curtain" calling the shots. Once again, his nurse picked up the phone. Again, she was told to "wait" by someone on the other end. Distressed Sam. Distressed Mom and Dad. He looked like he was going to have a heart attack, and we worried about what we knew was a real possibility—further damage to his brain. Unfortunately, we were the ones witnessing the assault on my son, but the person making the decision on whether or not to allow the turmoil to continue was making that decision from the other end of the phone. They were allowing the storm to continue based on reported numbers and a timed goal of fifteen minutes. The person holding the key, the person with the authority to make it all stop, was not in the room witnessing the distress that Sam was in. *Violent* is the only word I can use to describe it. Violent and terrifying!

Finally, on the third call, with around ten minutes of perilous territory behind us, Sam's nurse received permission to administer his Versed well before the fifteen-minute mark. She *ran* to the machine and pushed the button. Within seconds, the storm abated as his numbers returned to normal. His heart rate slowed. His chest cavity relaxed. No more heaving. No more spastic convulsions. There was a momentary reprieve from our fears and concerns only to propel us into the next crisis. As they examined Sam's eyes, they found them to be dilated once again—a clear indication that something negative was happening neurologically.

After paralyzing him with ROC, they rushed him downstairs for a CT scan once again to take more pictures of his poor brain. Just the trip for the picture was stressful on him as he was jostled to and fro. This whole fiasco threw him into another spiral of needing a tremendous amount of medication to keep him calm and bring his body back into a controlled state once again. The remainder of the day was spent trying to restore stability. As you might expect, the extubation did not happen.

Once he was back in his room and recovering from his trip, Sam's neurosurgeon came in to assure us that all was well. The CT showed increased swelling and several new bleeds, but nothing that was overly concerning for her. She explained how because the optic nerve had already been stretched out, it was highly susceptible to being affected again by any slight insult. They were all relieved to learn that the bleeds were minor, but I was not so consoled by the outcome. For all the many times I heard the phrase "equal, reactive and brisk" to describe Sam's eyes each and every time he was examined—hour upon hour, day and night for the past two weeks—following this storm, I never again heard those words to describe his eyes during exams. Objectively, Sam's eyes were affected, his brain was subjected to additional swelling, and several new bleeds were now evident on the CT scan. Other subjective changes happened that we all noticed but were difficult to quantify in his response to stimuli, but the effect this storm had on his eyes was sudden and drastic. It's impossible to know to what extent he was further injured, as we had no baseline of all his deficits prior to this storm. But the one thing we knew is that his eyes were once consistently "equal, reactive, and brisk"—and now they were no more.

Sam's team explained how they would need to put him back on his medications and come up with a new plan—a plan that involved bringing in a physiatrist to *wean* him from his current medications onto different medications. Medications that would still keep him safe but not in such a sedated state that would prohibit extubation.

For the first time since we stepped foot in the hospital, I was angry. On this road of Calvary, many negative emotions came and went. I experienced confusion, profound sadness, darkness, woundedness, disorientation, numbness, and defeat. These emotions would come, and they would go as they were always replaced by hope. But in all that time, I was never angry. I knew God too well and loved Him too much to be angry with Him. But tonight, I was angry—only it was not at God. I was angry that it happened. Angry at the staff that allowed it to happen. Angry at myself for not advocating for my son. Angry at their insistence that this was just a series of unfortunate events with no regard for the reality that we *caused* this series of events to unfold in the first place and that we chose to allow it to continue for ten minutes withholding useful medication. Now realizing that there was a Plan B and that Plan B was a much gentler option than Plan A, so much remorse flooded my heart. My son's already incredibly compromised brain was further subjected to more injury through this violent trial. And now, after the damage was already done, I was made aware that we had other options. Yes. I was indeed struggling with anger for the first time since we had arrived.

As we rounded the corner on that day, Sam had finally calmed back down. He was stable at last and once again on his Versed drip keeping things very steady and uneventful. The nurses were gently cleaning him up and tidying his bed for the evening. I watched as they lovingly cared for Sam, meticulously attending to every last detail to make him comfortable and to disturb him as little as possible. I began to let go of some of my anger. Nobody wanted to hurt Sam after all. Nobody tried to harm him. Even if it was a poor decision and not even a little logical to my mind, it wasn't done with malicious intent. The only reason Sam was even alive, after all, was completely due to the thousands of competent and careful decisions they had made thus far.

As my heart simmered down and peace was once again restored, one of the nurses looked beyond me out the large window to my back and exclaimed, "Oh! Look at the sky!"

As I turned around to look, my eyes met the most stunning and glorious sunset! It was truly magnificent and a fitting end to the dreariness that had been our companion all day! In that brief moment, a peace flooded my soul, letting me know that I could let it go. It was going to be okay. Tomorrow held the promise of good things.

CHAPTER 9

My 5:10

The days crawled by. Sam took to his new medications like a fish to water. They were able to successfully wean him from the potent cocktail that kept him sedated so as to attempt extubation once again. We delighted with each small step forward. No matter how tiny the victory, we celebrated hard. Each step in the right direction was dripping with promises of hope. Extubation—successful! Tracheotomy—not necessary! EEG leads—removed! Machines were untangled, disconnected, and removed from his bedside as the web of wires and medical interventions diminished by the day. The team meetings involved fewer and fewer personnel as discussions turned from survival to recovery. We began to discuss such hope-filled realities as when Sam would be moved from the PICU to the rehabilitation floor.

How ridiculously inadequate it is to say that the days passed by and then he graduated from the PICU. Minute by minute assessments of his progress. Desperate pleas to generate some sign of life from his lifeless body. Attempts to understand *if* he was responding and in what way. Learning to understand the catalyst of his storming episodes. Determining the cyclical nature of the storms and anticipating when they would brew up. The burden of acknowledging his utter helplessness as we assisted the nurses in changing the diapers of our eighty-pound infant. Unsuccessful attempts at placing boots on his feet in order to remedy his foot drop. Respiratory therapists placing vests on him periodically throughout the day and all hours of the night shaking him so that pneumonia would not settle in his chest. Inspecting his vacant eyes hour by hour as they shone lights directly in them eliciting no physical reaction in his body. Wound care. Sponge baths. Constant adjustments of his position in bed so as to encourage him to leave behind the fetal position and stretch his body out straight. Daily x-rays of his chest. Ports into his body failing and being removed. A PICC line inserted to do the job of all other entry points. Reflex checks. Moving from severe intolerance of touch to finally accepting my embrace. Minute by minute temperature fluctuations. Silent, dark nights wrapped in prayer as my white knuckles clung to my rosary beads at the bedside of my sleeping boy. The cumulative toll of these incremental minutes would eventually break even the strongest person if not for the hope-laced gifts sprinkled about. Gifts in the form of tangible progress as well as spiritual gifts sent from above. The spiritual gifts and consolations were innumerable. I have mentioned many already, but two others stand out in my memory from those early days.

A tremendous source of my suffering throughout this entire experience was the separation from my family—and my separation from Dave in particular. Even though Dave and I saw each other, it was generally to pass the torch or to converse about something that beckoned our attention in the moment. We would often sit in Sam's room watching numbers on a monitor or hanging on every reflexive movement he made. We were together but not connected. Taking care of business but disjointed. I would look at Dave, and all he was doing to keep our family afloat, all he was doing to keep life moving outside the walls of the PICU. And I had so much admiration for him because he was doing all those things that needed to be done but that I couldn't turn my attention to. And I had so much sadness for him. I realized he ached, and I couldn't help him any more than I could help myself. And I missed him.

And I ached for my children. Oh, how I missed them. My heart was in pieces to know that I couldn't be with them. I could not give them my time. I could offer them very little support. In the end, I really did not know how their hearts were holding up. I just prayed that when this was all said and done, that I would be able to pick up the pieces because this crisis was having a devastating impact on our family. We were going to be separated for a very long time. I did not know how long, and I didn't know what the repercussions would be. When I was at home with my other little ones, it would satisfy an ache in my heart to be with them to some degree, but it was burdened by my separation from Sam, burdened by my sheer exhaustion. I could not be any kind of a mom to them—other than to hug them and cuddle with them as I collapsed in my bed for the night. It was also burdened by a disconnect. We were living so much of life separated from one another that I didn't quite know how to enter their world once again when we were together. It was a strange feeling to be home, to be with my family, but to not feel a part of it. Each time I would plan a trip home to be with them, my heart would be in turmoil leading up to it. Especially in those early days in the hospital when Sam was so sick. I did not know what he was aware of. I did not know if he was afraid. My heart would break at the thought of leaving his world to go home for an evening, no matter how grateful I was to see my other children.

Thankfully, God always gave me a parting gift to console my heart and to let me know it would be alright. The first gift came in the PICU when Sam was unresponsive except for his motor response to reflex stimuli. As the hours crept by that day, I was anticipating the time when I would need to say goodbye and forcefully detach myself from Sam. I was experiencing much difficulty in coping with my separation from him, but I realized that my other children needed me too and I desperately missed them and so I resolved myself to doing this very painful thing that my entire being was resisting. Kissing him goodbye and walking out of his room to be home for the night. Finally, the moment arrived.

"Well, you better get going." Dave sensed that I needed a nudge to get myself in gear.

Tears filled my eyes as I walked over to Sam who was, as far as we could tell, still very much unconscious. I leaned down right next to his face and I said, "Sam, it's Mom." As I took a minute to get my composure, Sam's head turned ever so slightly in my direction. It was enough, though, to catch the attention of everyone in the room as they let out an audible gasp! Tears were rolling down my cheeks at this point as I choked out, "I love you so much. Do you know that I love you so much?"

By all accounts, Sam still appeared to be sleeping. His eyes were still very much closed. But even so, my sweet boy very meekly nodded his head up and down to tell me "yes." Oh, my heart! My son knows me! And he knows that I love him! I can't describe the elation in my heart to know that he heard me, that he responded to my voice, that he answered my question, that he knows my heart. Perhaps if he is afraid, perhaps my love for him can make him feel even just a little safer, and that was such a gift for me. Up until that moment, I had not been able to do even the slightest tangible thing to comfort my broken boy. Even in this exchange, I had to restrain myself and be content with our short interaction so that I did not put him at further risk. Even though this was a positive connection and exchange of love, it was enough to send all his numbers soaring. I kissed his cheek and backed away as they administered a rescue medication to calm his poor body down. But in this moment, I caught a glimpse of his heart. It was a glimpse of his *mind*, which had been sleeping so deeply since the day of his injury. It was a connection with my sweet Sam, and it was such a beautiful parting gift to help me as I detached to be with my other beautiful babies, to go home and connect with the hearts of my fourteen-year-old all the way down to my two-year-old.

As our community of family and friends rallied around us, many people would send encouraging words with a Scripture verse attached. These verses were often manna for my day and helped to keep my spirit in a hope-filled posture. Many were coincidental in their appearance. One message would be delivered by multiple people but always similar in nature. God knew what my heart needed that day, and He sent it to me through the hands and mouths of those around me, as well as through the daily Mass readings. There was one verse in particular, however, that became "our verse." A verse that my dear sister-in-law read and was struck by—and so shared with me.

And after you have suffered a little while, the God of all grace, who has called you to His eternal glory in Christ, will Himself restore, confirm, strengthen, and establish you (1 Peter 5:10)

On the surface, this verse is incredibly hope-filled. But it stands out from the various other verses sent our way for several reasons. First, it just *did*! It is impossible to understand the movements of our own hearts. When God speaks, He speaks! And it lands! And it sticks! And it won't let go of you. That is what this verse did. It landed and it was mine. Additionally, though, it was bathed in the sacred language of numerology. The book of first Peter reminded me of Sam's companions from Peter's Shadow who had diligently prayed for and over Sam from the beginning. But additionally, chapter 5, verse 10, 5:10, my birthday is May 10, and Sam went unconscious at about 5:10 p.m. My interest was piqued by those coincidences, but it was confirmed two months later when I had to agonizingly pull myself away from Sam to deliver our eighth baby. While our precious new addition was amazing and beautiful and wonderful, my labor and delivery experience was full of fear and weariness and defeat. My "5:10" came back to me when someone asked what time Henry was born. My dear husband, who is not typically so concerned with the details of such things, announced that our Henry entered the world at 5:10! It was consolation when I felt out of control. God-speak for "I've got this." God has, since then, called my attention to this number again and again. Often when I needed Him most.

I understood, from this Scripture verse, that it was His will that we go through this fire, that we embrace the cross that was custom crafted for us, but that we should hold onto the hope that we would be delivered from it ultimately. We would have to walk through this valley but that after we had suffered a little while, our God *would* restore, confirm, strengthen, and establish Sam specifically but our family collectively as well. I had the assurance that we would dance again one day. This was God's promise to me.

With this verse fresh in my mind, I awoke one day and spent a bit of time connecting with God through Scripture. The reading concerned the sacrifice of Abraham. At first glance, it touched me of course. But as I went to the reflection, I read this. "Because of the faith of Abraham, his son was restored to him." I stopped. I went no further because in that one sentence, my mind flashed back to consequential moments in my story. I saw that same thread that I had noticed before concerning my conversation with my sister a couple months prior when we were contemplating the nature of the story of Abraham. Grappling with the idea of offering your son. Grappling with our God who could ask such a sacrifice of us. I then thought about that moment after Mass when I had offered God a cracked door of surrender in offering to take the place of my dad and suffer for Him. I thought of Sam's name—"God has heard." I contemplated his birth. Sam was the only one of my (at the time) seven children who was born without my water breaking in advance. I was curiously ignored by the nurses throughout the night as I expressed that I felt I was getting close to transition. By the time they took me seriously and checked to see how I was progressing, my little one was on his way out, and my water broke only as he was being delivered. I understood that this was protection for his little head, as it was not yet time for us to be handed our cross. I considered the providential timing of the accident and how Sam really shouldn't even be with us, how it should have been far more devastating, and how we were protected from that. And I contemplated my journey over the past three years as I have gotten to know my God. My time spent strengthening that umbilical in preparation for the trial that awaited me. And then I considered that I hadn't abandoned my God for even a moment as I was traveling this road. "Because of the faith of Abraham, his son was restored to him." Because of my faith, Sam was going to be restored to me. Not because of anything I did or did not do and not because my faith was all that admirable or amazing, but only because that was God's will for us. Because of my faith, I could rest assured that God's will would be done. And in this moment, I understood that it was God's holy will that Sam should be restored to us. I did not understand how that would look. A miraculous instantaneous healing? Restored completely or partially? I did not know. I only knew that "Sam" would be restored to me. My son would come back.

Little by little by very little, Sam became stronger and healthier. He was able to detach from the PICU umbilical after around three weeks. His vent was out. He was disconnected from many of his machines with only a small entourage of mechanical friends following him to his new home on 7100. It all seemed too soon in my estimation. We had been completely dependent on the PICU staff to keep our son alive for the past three weeks, and it felt entirely reckless to abandon their care. He still seemed so fragile after all. He was still "sleeping" and looked quite vulnerable as they said their goodbyes. His team assured me that he *is* getting better and that he really needs to move on to rehabilitation to begin the work of restoration.

Restore
Confirm
Strengthen
Establish

Yes, we had our work cut out for us. It was time to begin. We had suffered a little while. Now was the time for God to show His hand as He worked and we worked to restore our Sam.

CHAPTER 10

Born Again

We took our newborn Sam up to his new home on 7100. He slept constantly, much like a newborn. He didn't even wake up to eat, as his "nose straw" was doing that work for him. The work of therapy began before his eyes were even open. This looked very much like taking a baby fresh from the womb and having him press on an iPad or practice sitting up straight—an exercise in futility. Initially, the medical staff was not aware that he was awake because his eyes were firmly closed. But when they made their rounds, we helped them to understand that he was actually awake and aware, that he only appeared to be sleeping. We knew this because he would respond to us without opening his eyes. He would move a bit upon request while seemingly remaining asleep. As the rehab staff entered the room, they gently sat Sam up in his bed. His head had all the control of a day-old baby. They placed their hands under his chin to help him do the impossible. You could see in the expression on Sam's face that he was really trying to assist in holding his head up, though in reality his musculature was about as effective as a wet noodle. His raised eyebrows were the only signs of life expressing that he had a desire to open his eyes—a desire to hold up his head. He just could not do it.

Our baby Sam went through his oral fixation all over again as he chewed on everything compulsively. We bought him a "chewie" to wear around his neck as his poor soggy, wrinkled fingers were taking the brunt of this fixation. As he woke up to the world around him, he became incredibly attached to mama once again as you might expect one to do when newly born for the second time. This attachment to his mom continued well past when we went home from the hospital months later. His left side emerged in the very same position you would find a newborn limb. Spastic and fetal. It did not occur to me to consider these observations very deeply at first. But I would learn later that these observations and comparisons of Sam to an infant fresh from the womb would serve me well as we progressed in his therapy many months later. In the moment, I observed. Then I placed those observations in my pocket as I gave the therapists free reign to do as they wished in bringing Sam back to us.

The therapists were confident that they could get him walking within a couple months, which tickled my own ambitions for him. A walking Sam is closer to the Sam in my memory than a wheelchair Sam. And so yes! Please get him walking again! And quick! Botox and casts? A plastic orthotic? Sure! You need to work him hard to get results? Yes! Please do so! We only have a window of six months to a year of rapid recovery before the dreaded plateau? Yes! Push him hard and make the most of it! I was completely on board with everything they were suggesting was necessary. *It was tough.*

Our days were full of Botox and casting, plastic orthosis and bathroom catastrophes. Many, many tears were shed as Sam became incredibly frustrated by all that was being asked of him. Hold your head up, open your eyes, tall kneel, reach up high, electrical stim, doctors' evaluations, poking, prodding. Therapy all day long six days per week—all being done with half of his skull missing. Occasionally, Sam's tears and groanings would escalate to an angry rage as he released his frustration in the face of one of his therapists. This was so difficult to watch because it was not the Sam I knew. My Sam was so laid back, so go-with-the-flow. This Sam who was defiant and frustrated and so prone to fits was a very different person than who I knew. But additionally, it was difficult because I understood the gravity of what they were asking him to do. It often looked like torture as he figured out how to be aware of and move his body once again. And to a certain extent, it worked! Therapy made Sam strong again, and the therapists that worked him the hardest got the best results.

At first, Sam was in a full-body wheelchair. He could not hold his head up and fell continuously to the side if not supported. His eyes were still closed for the most part as he went about his day. At one point, probably around a month into this journey, we were getting into the elevator following a therapy session. The therapist was escorting us back up to Sam's room for a break. In the elevator with the three of us was a mother and her sweet little boy. He looked at Sam and then nervously scooted closer and grabbed his mother's hand. She offered us an uncomfortable smile as the small box climbed slowly upward; the awkward exchange hung thick in the air. Remembering my once whole and healthy Sam—and now noticing the dichotomy of this sweet, healthy, but uncomfortable little boy next to our reality, which was our son in a full-body chair, missing his skull, wearing a helmet, minimally conscious with his eyes still closed, unable to talk—I just could not hold myself together. I had been so strong for so long, and the floodgates could no longer hold back the hysterics. I tried desperately to at least wait until we were off the elevator, but I just couldn't.

As the tears started to flow, the kind lady must have been so grateful that mercifully the doors opened so she could remove herself and her son. We traveled further upwards as the tears and snot just poured out of me in uncontrollable sobs. As we arrived back in Sam's room, his therapist attempted to communicate with me. All I could do was open a photo album of Sam prior to his injury. I could say nothing because I was completely undone, but I just pounded on a picture of my Sam with my pointer finger. She understood and said, "I get it. That is your son. This is not him." I shook my head yes and then managed to assure her I would be fine. She hurried out after getting Sam situated back in his bed. I climbed in beside him and just cried. Until that moment, I had tried so hard to be strong for him. I tried to never cry in front of him, even when I was sure he was not aware. But now, knowing that he was probably aware, nonetheless, I let it flow.

As I lay there next to Sam, I bawled. I was able to tell him that I was just so sad, that I felt so badly that he had to go through this, that I would take his place in a moment if I could, that I wanted so badly to make it all go away for him. I told him that it was okay if he felt sad too. I looked at him, and a single tear rolled down his cheek. We just laid there in bed in the dark, my arms wrapped around him. And we cried. It was beautiful and awful and precious.

After allowing this explosion of emotion, I got myself together and felt a renewed strength to move forward. Apologizing to Sam for his "crazy mother," I assured him we would get through it, that I would be with him the whole time and that it would be okay. I explained how one day we would be back home together, and he would be strong and healthy. Having released my pent-up emotions, we were ready to move on and to begin our afternoon sessions. Before heading out, however, someone from psychology came in to check on "Sam." Something tells me they were a little concerned about the crazy lady in the elevator.

Our weeks continued on. Sam continued to awaken. Eventually he learned to talk again which is an amazing and precious memory. It was even more exhilarating than when he said even his *first* "first word" as a small child. We had been working with him for a while, but he had been unable to produce any sound as of yet. One day, Dave was inspired to ask him to say "hi"—which was an excellent choice of words because of how breathy it is. Sam was finally able to say "Hhhhhhhhhhhiiiiiii" in the teeniest little voice. Oh, how we rejoiced! Shortly after, he could say, "No." Before long—as in, literally, a few days later—the family came in to visit Sam. It happened to be our sweet Amelia's thirteenth birthday. At this point, we were about a month out from his injury. With his small weak voice that had managed to say only one-syllable words until then, Sam sang a very sweet rendition of "Happy Birthday" to serenade his sister. We were all in tears to see him returning to us little by little.

A memory that I will forever hold dear involved a moment when Sam was lying in bed resting between therapy sessions. I had the lights dimmed trying to coax him into a slumber to get some much-needed rest. In those days, it was often very difficult to understand anything Sam was trying to say because his voice was so incredibly weak. His words were only partially formed, and so we had to guess as to what he wanted to communicate.

As he lay there in his bed, he was repeating the same words again and again. It sounded almost like a rhyme as I could discern a certain cadence to his efforts. I listened a couple of times but could not figure out what he was trying to say. I didn't want to ask for clarification because I really just wanted him to go to sleep. He had been working so hard, and without sleep, he became really quite emotional due to cognitive fatigue. The very same words escaped his mouth again and again. Finally, I was too curious to wait any longer, and so I asked him if he was reciting a poem. He shook his head no. I asked if it was a song. "Yes." Okay. We're getting closer.

I asked if it was a VBS song because he loved those so much. "Yes." Ah-ha! A VBS song, okay!

Was it a song from VBS last year? "No." Interesting!

Was it a song from VBS this year? "Yes!"

So, I went to my laptop and pulled up *VBS songs 2018* and very quickly deciphered what he was trying to sing! Just listen!

Through every storm of life, I know you're by my side
So, I am holding on to your promises
You are the God who holds my future, all my dreams
So, I am holding on. You never let go of me!

You gave me hope when hope was all but gone
A second chance to sing a brand-new song
You opened up my eyes to see
You rescued me, You rescued me

You showed the way when there was no way out
Cleared up my mind when you erased all doubt
You made me strong when I was weak
You rescued me, You rescued me!

You are my God; I'm holding onto you.
You are my God; I know you'll see me through.
You are my God; I'm holding onto you.
You are my God; I know you'll see me through. Hey!

My son! My son! My son who was supposed to struggle with vocabulary deficits and memory deficits, my son who was supposed to have a lapse in his memory for *at least* a few days to weeks before his stroke—he remembered word for word the song that he had learned in only two days at VBS, including the very morning of the day that he was afflicted! This would be quite an accomplishment for *any* child after only two days of instruction but *especially* for someone with a fresh brain injury! God helped him to learn this very important song, and then nestled it very deeply in his consciousness so that he could retrieve it when he would most need it! He was communicating with Sam and consoling his heart just the same as He was consoling mine! I shed quite a few tears of praise and thanksgiving before picking my jaw up off the floor to return to therapy.

That is how things went. Painful moments mixed with sweet memories mixed with great rejoicing in even the smallest of victories. Somewhere along the way, Sam was able to graduate to a mixture of tube feedings mixed with a light diet of pureed foods and thickened liquids. Occasionally, he would look out the window at the end of the hallway to see the Rubber Ducks baseball game. Mostly, his "outings" involved going down to the patio and gardens outside the hospital. We would lift Sam out of his chair and lay him in the green grass to feel the sunshine and fresh air. We felt incredibly grateful to be stuck in the hospital during the summer so that he could escape a bit here and there.

Sam had been without his skull for around eight weeks. Unless you have experience in this department, I'm not sure you can imagine how disturbing this is. The right half of Sam's head had virtually no protection over his brain. Depending on Sam's position and where the fluid deposited itself at the moment, his head would take on different shapes. Occasionally, it would be nice and round as the fluid would be evenly distributed. Often, though, his head would reveal the reality that he only had half a skull. His left side would be a beautiful round globe, and then right around the stitches, there would be a sharp "drop-off" where the bone ended. The entire right side of his head would reveal a gruesome flat slope.

Worse was when Sam would have an itch on that side of his head. As you can imagine, each time he would reach up to scratch his itchy healing wound, we would have to slap his hand away. It was a futile effort, however, and so we ended up giving him a cloth to keep with him at all times. He learned to use this cloth to reach up and ever so gently rub his gelatinous head. After around eight weeks of this, Sam was ready to go back into surgery to have his bone replaced. They were keeping it on ice just waiting for him to be ready. I have never been so excited at the prospect of one of my kids going under the knife. We were so grateful to finally have him restored. It is dangerous business to walk around and work in therapy without a skull even if he did wear a helmet, but it was also simply very disturbing to look at. We were ready to see him whole again.

Sam went into surgery and emerged just fine. It was, however, our first glimpse at the effects of traumatic stress. His fresh wound looked very similar to his first surgery. His swollen face and puffy eyes looked identical to the ordeal we had just "recovered" from. Dave and I were both completely blindsided by our emotions as Sam appeared to have gone back to the starting gate. We logically knew that this was a blip in the radar, and we would soon be on the other side, but post-traumatic stress is not interested in logic. It takes you places, emotionally, that you do not choose.

As they wheeled him through the large doors toward surgery, we found ourselves disproportionately traumatized by visions of his first trip through those doors. As his fresh stitches traced the same familiar path on his head and his face and eyes swelled in the aftermath, we found ourselves struggling to maintain our trust. It was as if we were in the ring. We had endured the blows as they came and even felt a bit stronger day by day, but as we were still staggering, a final blow was delivered landing us on the ground. It was probably one of our lowest moments spiritually. We did not expect to be anything but happy that he was going to have a bone over his brain again. But we found ourselves shaking our fist just a little at God, asking how much more He was going to throw at Sam. He endured three days of therapy in complete darkness as his red, shiny eyes were both swollen entirely shut. At one point during therapy, however, my son sat on the edge of the table and endeared himself to his therapists surrounding him.

"Oh Sam…you're so sweet! Can I take you home with me?"

My little blind Sam, in a tiny little voice, with his stiff upper lip quivering so as not to cry replied, "No, thank you. I have a pretty great mom already." Oh, my heart!

After day three, his eyes began to peek open little by little. He had been wrestling with a fever that was being treated with Tylenol. By this time, it was climbing and a bit more difficult to manage. They were watching it closely to make sure it was not an infection setting in from surgery. They had drawn a line in what they would tolerate. At around ten or eleven at night, Sam crossed this arbitrary line, and a team of medical professionals descended upon him like a swarm of locusts. They were compelled to run a whole battery of tests on Sam to figure out the source of the infection. An attempted blood draw. Unsuccessful. A second attempt. Unsuccessful. After a third painful but successful stick of the needle, my desperate Sam could finally relax a bit.

It was then explained that they needed a urine sample and so he would need to endure a catheter. "No worries, though. The hard part is over. This will just feel like pressure, but it will not be painful." I will tell you: they were very wrong. I had to pry Sam off the ceiling when they were finished. I assure you: it was far worse than the three painful attempts at a blood draw. Two different people and two different-sized straws later, they were finally able to retrieve the sample they were after. I'm not sure if the pain was truly that intense or if Sam's newly acquired acute sensitivity to pain was to blame, but my poor Sam could be heard screaming through the closed door. This whole ordeal was pretty traumatic for both of us. His slumber was abruptly interrupted by bright lights. A team of strangers in white coats. Needles. Pokes. Pain. Thankfully, Sam has no recollection of this experience. There were more than a few traumatic moments that reduced both of us to tears that, even to this day, Sam does not recall. Ports removed. Staples in. Staples out. Blood draws. Botox injections. Many, many moments that should have left a negative impression, and yet, most of them are long forgotten.

Thankfully, Sam had no infection. It turned out to be a pretty common reaction to the temporary synthetic dura layer that was in his head from the surgery. His body was experiencing an inflammatory response to this foreign object. We needn't worry as the synthetic layer would dissolve and be replaced (hopefully) by some semblance of a natural dura layer.

So went our experience with recovery. Painful wounds. Sweet memories. Battle scars that we will always have but that ultimately have become a part of our story—a part of us. Precious memories that I will carry with me forever. Watching Dave pick Sam up out of his bed, set him lovingly in his wheelchair, and place his helmet on his head to wheel him down to the gift shop to purchase the newspaper. Taking Sam outside for "pudding dates." Finding reasons to smile and laugh during our long days. Seeing Sam open his eyes just a bit and wave for the first time when his cousins came for a visit. Tucking his feeding tube into his helmet to keep it up out of the way as we went on our excursions. Buying big-kid camo pull-ups for our newborn Sam to help him feel a bit better about his current situation in the hospital diapers. Comforting cups of coffee. Hospital ice chips. The same selection of movies on the hospital TV day after day. The bedside remote getting lost under covers. Daily food orders for breakfast, then lunch, then dinner. The daily trips to the cafeteria for my own sustenance when grandparents were visiting Sam. Hospital showers. Couch beds night after night. Surgeries that came and went and came and went. Scans of Sam's brain that came and went and came and went. Tense moments of unexpected complications. Staples removed. New incisions. Staples removed once again. Ports and drains. Fluid collection bulbs. PT and OT and Speech therapy. Music therapy, art therapy and the Doggy Brigade. Full body wheelchair and then his normal wheelchair. Botox and casts and casts and casts and then, finally, his leg brace. My dad's surgery for his prostate cancer came and went. Tears and tears and more tears. Some for sadness. Others for joy. And still others for painfully hard work. Prayer after prayer. Anointing after anointing. Rosary after rosary.

One night, around eleven, as I was sitting by my son's bedside, I received a text from a friend of mine. "You'll never guess where I am right now." As it turns out, she was in the ER with her son. I told her I would be down to visit with her as Sam was fast asleep.

As I ventured out of our room into the quiet dark halls of the hospital, I noticed an odd familiarity as I went on my way. Walking the dark halls of a largely abandoned hospital in the middle of the night should be a bit disconcerting. But instead, it felt as familiar as walking around in my own home in the middle of the night. My path was clear and sure as I padded down the long corridors in my pajamas and slippers. The only disturbance in my thoughts as I traveled was the thought of how odd it was that I should feel such comfort in my surroundings. Just me, pacing the halls of my temporary home.

Time marched onward, and life refused to wait for us. Our eighth child entered the world while Sam was still in the hospital. Little Henry Alexander was named by Sam as he reemerged from his slumber and found his voice again. As Sam anxiously awaited my return from his bed at Children's Hospital, I lay in my own bed a block away at General Hospital. My weary and defeated body approached labor and delivery with much trepidation. It is a tough thing to go into labor already defeated. It seems to me that one must have at least a little fight in them to cope with the demands of labor. I had nothing left to give, and it felt terrifying and out of control.

Ultimately, Henry was born without a hitch, and he was beautiful and precious and amazing. Upon his arrival, I made sure to send Dave away to tend to Sam and the other children, and so Henry and I sat in complete silence and relative darkness for two days. My spirit could not tolerate such mindless distractions as the television or the internet. My mind could not tolerate the demands of something as simple as reading. It was as if I was very much on "empty" and needed to recharge. I needed silence, quiet, darkness, introspection, cuddles, solitude, stillness—in order to examine my spirit, to reorient myself in my world, to restore some kind of homeostasis, to rekindle my conversation with my God. For two days, Henry and I sat there together, staring at one another in the dim light of the hospital room. Those days were heavy with sadness but mixed with a quiet joy.

I took my two days and then joined the race once again. But this time with "my hands behind my back" as I could not offer as much tangible assistance to Sam while holding our newborn. Henry lived his first two weeks of life at the hospital that we had called home for close to two months. We began to take short field trips off the hospital grounds to practice "handling" Sam on our own. We looked forward to August 31 when Sam could come home with us for good.

After seventy-three days in the hospital, our homecoming was not as I could have anticipated it on day one of our journey. Sam's shoes that were handed to us in the plastic bag the night of his trauma were not a monument to our dead son after all. But he also did not wear them out of the hospital as his new orthotic would not fit in a normal tennis shoe. Our destiny lay somewhere in the middle. The boy they gave back to us was a bit different than who we brought in. This boy did not walk. He leaned perpetually to the side drooling out the corner of his mouth. His processing speed and speech were very slow, and he was incredibly prone to emotional outbursts from minute to minute. This boy coming home with us stuttered mercilessly, and his right eye was drifting completely to the side.

In addition to the reality of who we were left with, I was also caught unaware by my difficulty in detaching from our hospital home. As I was packing up all the cards, gifts, prayer cards, rosaries, oil, medals, blankets, pillows, toys and snacks that we had accumulated, and I noticed the room becoming more and more empty, I began to find myself very disturbed by this momentous occasion. I had longed for this day when we could go home and be together again. But I was realizing that our "happily ever after" was looking much different than I had anticipated.

As we closed the door to our temporary home and ushered Sam out of the hospital to return to life, I was keenly aware that we were nowhere close to the finish line. We had endured seventy-three days in the hospital. We had walked through hell and made it to the glorious day of his homecoming. But I realized that for all the work we did, for all we had endured, for the incredible toll it had taken on us, we were still only at the starting gate. This boy we were bringing home with us was a very different person than the one we brought in two and a half months prior. There was much work left to do. There was an incredible road that still remained in front of us—work to do in the realm of therapy and restoration, work to do in the realm of grief and acceptance, work to do in the realm of hope and faith, and work to do in restoring our entire family.

Sam came home to a yard full of loved ones with signs and balloons honking their car horns, hooting and hollering. And then we went inside. And the crowd left us. And we realized we were terrified at our new reality. Eight children looking to us for their education and sustenance. A newborn baby demanding much of my time and attention. Our Sam who simply couldn't walk or ambulate from couch or bed to bathroom. Bladders that simply had no capacity for "in a minute." Our once bubbly and independent Sam was now as dependent as a newborn baby.

Without motivation and an incredible amount of assistance, his default was to sit on the couch, unengaged with anyone or anything around him—simply existing but wasting away unless we intervened. Our family fell apart. The baby and the toddler were perpetually screaming as their needs were not being met. Our eldest son was processing everything in his own way, which meant he completely disconnected from the family. He just checked out and had no patience for anyone or anything. Every bit of noise and chaos grated on his nerves and sent him into isolation every chance he got. Our girls suffered the weight of our incompetence as parents and found themselves with more responsibility than children their age should have to endure. Matters of faith began to drive a wedge between Dave and I as he struggled to understand a God who would do this to his son. We were broken. Badly.

People would often encourage us with words such as "I'll bet you are so glad to have Sam home with the whole family again." I would offer a smile and simply nod "yes." We were not happy. Not even close. We were a mess. We had no idea how we would ever be able to manage all these little people again. In contemplating our life decisions such as remaining open to life as our family grew and grew and contemplating our decision to keep the kids home for their education, I couldn't help but notice that *something* had to give! "You've got the wrong girl!" I would lament. "I simply can't do all you are asking of me!" How would we ever find our happiness or joy again. Our entire family was in a very dark pit—existing together but expressing very little love. Doing what was on the checklist for the day, but grating on each other's nerves as we all strove to simply stay afloat.

Dave's strength in attending to all the details of life was remarkable. I could not force my mind to attend to any thoughts or tasks beyond Sam. It was really Dave that kept life moving forward. He did the grunt work of finding a buyer for our store and negotiating a deal. He was the one that dotted all the *i*'s as we figured out the million and one details of a business transfer. Thankfully, the buyer was a Godsend. A very good man with a good heart and a sincere desire to make it as easy as possible for us. Bills were paid, and life continued thanks to the attention of my husband. I could do one thing and one thing only—focus on Sam and his recovery.

As Dave sank deeper and deeper into a spiritual pit, however, I would often envision our family all floating on the sea. Everyone was treading water and in danger of going under spiritually speaking. I was doing my best to keep everyone afloat and bounce them back up once they began to succumb to their weariness, all while perilously close to going under myself. I would offer words of encouragement in an attempt to "bounce" Dave back up, but he didn't want my encouragement. He resisted my assistance and was even resentful that I should try to help him "swim." And then I would grow angry at his resistance but also his unwillingness to help me with the other kids in their faith journeys. At any moment, everyone would go down at once, and I would drown due to the weight of trying to keep everyone else afloat. We really were hanging on by a thread.

We were home. But we still "lived" at the hospital. Sam's therapy was seven hours per day/five days per week. This didn't include his constant appointments with all of his various doctors—physiatry, neurology, neurosurgery, epileptology, neuropsychology, ophthalmology, optometry, not to mention his PCP. Our days were hard and without joy. Sam was very emotional as they worked him so very hard during his sessions. Additionally, there was a constant struggle between our newborn Sam needing his mother to be with him and the "encouragement" from therapists to disconnect so as to foster his independence. To heap pain on top of pain, I was still disconnected from my other children most of the time in order to attend to Sam.

Despite our bleak existence, the rays of the sun would still shine on us from time to time. One day in particular, we had canceled our therapy sessions in the morning in order to attend a medical appointment. I awoke very early to begin my day. Between tending to the constant needs of Henry, I managed to get myself showered and ready. I woke Sam up and began the long process of assisting him in getting ready. It is worth mentioning at this point that Sam's processor was not up to speed. His every move was sloth-like. Conversations were painfully slow. His movements were at a snail's pace. Trips to the bathroom could take twenty minutes—and were only successful around fifty percent of the time. All of this while tending to the needs of a newborn.

After numerous attempts in the bathroom, a couple of diaper changes, a couple nursing sessions, we left the house very late. When we arrived at the doctor's office in the pouring rain, I muscled our now ninety-pound Sam out of our very tall van, situated him in his wheelchair, and proceeded to put Henry in his stroller. I had no hand for an umbrella, and so I pushed the wheelchair with one hand and pulled the stroller with the other as the rain pelted our heads, causing Sam to cry with an audible groan. We spilled into the waiting room absolutely dripping wet around fifteen minutes late. Out of breath, I made my way to the counter only to be told apologetically that I would need to reschedule. I was too exhausted and upset to head right back out into the rain, and so I sat my defeated body in the chair and filled out the paperwork anyway so that we would be ready for the next attempt.

As I sat there filling out the paperwork, Sam—who now had the patience of a two-year-old—peppered me with questions on whether or not we could leave. For his slow processing speed, his questions came like a broken record. Relentless and always dissatisfied with my answers.

Trying to hide my emotions, I sat with my head down as I filled out the paperwork. Occasionally the tears I was trying to hide would escape and land on the papers in my lap. With laser focus to accomplish at least this one task today, I missed the announcement when the nurse called out, "Sam Lile?"

It wasn't lost on Sam, however. "Did they call my name?"

I looked up, and again the kind lady asked, "Sam Lile?"

"Yes," I answered, utterly perplexed. I stood up and began to ask what happened. She explained that another patient had given up her appointment for Sam! Even now, it brings tears to my eyes to contemplate this angel and the difference she made in our day. Her selfless gesture brings a warmth even now that inspires me to do better in recognizing and meeting the needs of others.

This journey, and all of the trials that came with it, has led us to encounter some of the most amazing people. We have been richly blessed by friends and strangers alike, people that we happened to meet that could relate to our journey and offer us some manna—medical personnel, patients and their families, strangers with similar life journeys, an entire community of people praying us right through and offering us tangible help when we most needed it. The Body of Christ has never been so tangible to me as it has been in the past couple years as our stories and paths have intertwined with the paths of others creating a tapestry that is incredibly intricate and yet impossible to fully comprehend or appreciate this side of heaven.

CHAPTER 11

Spiritual Threads

In addition to Sam's usual appointments with various medical professionals, we also began a relationship with an unorthodox MD up in Westlake, Ohio. Dr. Isaam Nemeh had been suggested to us by a friend, and it was the first time I had heard of him. Under the inspiration of the Holy Spirit, I decided to go ahead and make that appointment. This medical doctor is also known for the miraculous healings that take place under his care. It is a well-kept secret that heaven appears to touch down in his humble office as he employs his unconventional medical treatments including Meridian Regulatory Acupuncture.

We were told by Dr. Nemeh that Sam was receiving a healing at that first appointment, but it did not seem to extend beyond his bladder function. His normally spastic bladder was suddenly able to tolerate the "wait a minute" after that initial appointment. This gift was a game changer for a mom who was at the constant mercy of little bladders in general.

The larger gift that we received that day, however, involved Sam's dad. Dave arrived at the appointment with a palpable anger. Dr. Nemeh's wife picked up on it instantly. As soon as he entered the waiting room and headed for the bathroom, Kathy exclaimed, "Oh my! His attitude!"

I nodded and said that he was a bit skeptical.

Kathy reassured me, "No worries. It will be fine. You sit next to Sam."

In the middle of the appointment, Henry could be heard crying in the waiting room. Dave, from the far end of the long room, asked if I needed to get him. Sam echoed Dave's sentiment that I should attend to Henry. I replied that I would give him a minute. My mom was with him, and I was hoping that he would settle for her. But Dr. Nemeh looked up from his work, looked me straight in the eye, and said, "The baby needs you."

Sensing in his words a prompting of the Spirit, I stood up right away and excused myself. I went out to tend to Henry briefly, and upon returning, I found Dave sitting in the seat next to Sam with a completely different and light-hearted demeanor! Kathy told me on our way out that Dave seemed so different than when we first arrived and that she had been outside praying for him the entire time. God's gift to us at this appointment was a healing for Dave. His heart was softened and now open to receive the graces that God wanted to give him through this journey. Until this moment, he was becoming increasingly angry, disconnected, and growing weary of me. But from that moment on, our household began to heal.

You know, in Scripture, *Samuel* was the one who anointed *David*, the unlikely leader of Israel. In considering Sam's life journey over the years, it would seem that there is a very strong spiritual connection between Dave and his son. Dave joined the Church and was baptized the very same year that Sam was born and baptized into the faith. Additionally, for whatever reason, Dave never received his First Reconciliation after joining the Catholic faith. Eight years later, child after child received their initial sacraments, and Dave never opted to join in despite my encouragement to do so. It wasn't until *Sam* made his First Reconciliation that Dave decided (without my prompting or encouragement) to receive this sacrament alongside his son.

They both entered the confessional with a young priest named Fr. Jacob Bearer. This priest was none other than the one who came to our side at the hospital to anoint Sam when he entered his passion. He was a visiting priest at our parish and really did not know us at all but somehow ended up at the bedside of Sam in the hospital. We had very little connection to Fr. Bearer up until that point, but through this journey, he has become a very important part of our story and our lives. A thread of spiritual camaraderie connecting Dave with Sam has run throughout their lives. And it has been through Sam's affliction, his cross, his journey, that Dave was pulled out of his complacency and skepticism of the faith and brought into a deeper union with God.

We returned to Dr. Nemeh's office multiple times, and each time we received some good gift. It began with Dave and then our marriage and then finally a healing for the entire family. The most profound experience in his office came one evening when we brought the entire family with us (plus, grandparents to help with the youngest two littles). In hindsight, I am surprised that I would have taken advantage of the good doctor's time in this way as we have a large family. It didn't occur to me to even consider it until we were gently reprimanded just a bit by his staff. It was indeed thoughtless of me, but I really do plead ignorance and guidance by the Spirit.

Dr. Nemeh came out into the waiting room to see the family spilled about everywhere. In his customary way of gentleness and love, he began praying for people one by one, and we began witnessing God's love pouring down on us again and again. My eldest son, the one who had become quite disconnected and grumpy in general, went home a changed guy. His anger was gone. He was communicating with the family. He no longer moped about with a furrowed brow. His joy had returned, and everyone noticed it!

The doctor walked over to Dave and put his hand directly on the area of Dave's arm that had been painful for quite some time. A gentle touch. A silent prayer…and healed! He nearly stumbled into my dad as he landed with his hand on his back alleviating his sciatica.

Next, Dr. Nemeh got down on his knee and looked at Julianne (my little prophetess). Julianne is such a mixture of an angelic nature mixed with darkness that confounds me often. She has seen angels. She has spoken many prophetic messages to me that have made my jaw drop. But her temper! Whew! And her seeming perception of dark forces that terrify her at night is more pronounced than the other kids leading us into prayer to calm her spirit quite often. And so I had to smile when Dr. Nemeh looked at her and said, "She has a very strong spirit!"

I nodded.

He chuckled and said, "She is a good girl." It was almost as if he was acknowledging her double nature but assuring me that I need not worry.

The most miraculous gift of all came when he stood next to Sarah and Claire. I brought them to him together because they were both dealing with the same affliction. They had both suffered from constant bladder infections for many years. I don't say chronic because that would imply that there were periods of time when they were well. Not so. They were infected one hundred percent of the time. Sarah had been through two different surgeries over the years in an attempt to remedy her reflux from her bladder to her kidneys. Her kidneys had been damaged in the process of enduring these infections. She had been on prophylactic antibiotics for years. They did not work and left her sicker than when she began. We were finally able to break the vicious cycle of illness and antibiotics through a natural remedy called D-Mannose. This supplement kept the infections low grade so that they did not make her sick for the most part, but it never got rid of them completely. If you ran a test at any given time, you would find both of them infected. Always. We were told that based on Sarah's affliction that all of her siblings would have a 50/50 chance of being afflicted in the same way. And so when Claire began showing signs of infection at the age of three, we were not surprised. Much like Sarah, she was not helped by antibiotics. We didn't even consider the surgery for her as it failed us twice with Sarah. We just began a regimen of D-Mannose and tried to keep her minimally infected as much as we could. Because of these infections in our eleven and seven-year-old, we were buying diapers or pull-ups for Sarah, Sam, Claire, Michael, and now Henry. Additionally, the odor of urine that is infected with bacteria is incredibly potent and foul smelling. Our house had been a constant battleground for odors due to pull-ups that didn't make it to the trashcan or that leaked onto sheets in the middle of the night or a couch that was sat on before changing into fresh clothes. This was no minor affliction. It was a thorn each and every day for the past nine years. I had begged God again and again to heal them. It seems he was saving that moment for such a time as this. Until this moment, God's answer had always been "no"—or at least "not yet." Each and every singular morning, for as long as we could remember, Sarah and Claire would both bring their pull-ups up to the trashcan absolutely dripping wet. Completely saturated. Especially poor Sarah. Claire would have the occasional dry night, but Sarah was never so fortunate. Not once. This was becoming a problem for the young lady she now was. No eleven-year-old wants to rely on pull-ups at night.

As Dr. Nemeh moved next to Sarah, his hand went right for her neck as he said, "She has a neck injury!" I thought perhaps he misunderstood me as I was explaining her bladder problems. He confirmed, "No, that's what it is! A neck injury!" He began rubbing her neck with his hands very gently and said, "It is getting better." A little more rubbing, and again, "It is moving."

He then moved to Claire, and before he even touched her neck, he exclaimed, "Hers is much worse!" Again, he rubbed her neck gently. Again, he consoled us that "It is moving." As we looked back to the days when their problems began, we remembered that Sarah had fallen down the stairs and knocked out her tooth not long before her infections began. Claire had slipped in the bathtub and needed stitches in her chin just prior to her problems. It seems that both girls had a very serious injury due to the whiplash they sustained. Who would have thought that this affliction that was supposedly hereditary in the family was actually due to two completely isolated and unrelated incidents?

On one hand, I believed in miracles. That was the whole reason we went to see Dr. Nemeh in the first place. But as I was confronted by this possibility that my daughters were perhaps receiving a miraculous healing, I found myself confounded and a bit skeptical. At this point, I realized that I shouldn't have taken advantage of the doctor's time in this way, and so I did not ask for anything for myself. I quickly thanked him and packed everyone up to head home. We went to bed.

The next morning, Sarah and Claire both exclaimed that they were dry when they awoke! "Okay!" I said. It was highly unlikely that they would both be dry, but I wasn't ready to shout Hallelujah just yet and so I suppressed my giddy optimism. That day, their necks hurt them quite badly all day long. This, too, was unlikely as Dr. Nemeh's touch was so gentle. But they both felt as if things continued to move. Morning number two, dry! Morning number three, dry! Morning number four, dry again! By this time, Dave had already headed south to Florida with the older kids as I lagged behind for our flight with Sam and the littles. We were to meet up with the older kids by flying out the next day. I couldn't leave, however, without saying thank you.

The day of our flight, I made the drive up to Westlake again in the morning. I felt compelled to thank them for giving their time, for the work that they do, for being a conduit of God's love for us. I delivered some chocolate-covered strawberries to the staff and a card thanking them for the good fruits that came from our appointment. I explained how I now realized how inappropriate it was to bring everyone up for this appointment; however, I could only explain it by being blinded by the Spirit so that He could heal our entire family. The day following this amazing appointment, I was listening to a podcast about Dr. Nemeh called Blind Faith Live. In that podcast, Kathy expressed how sometimes "entire families need healing." This was confirmation for me that it was God who led us there. Our entire family *did* need to be healed. And God did not disappoint in pouring out His love on all of us. That entire month when we were in Florida, the girls remained one hundred percent dry! Dave and I were astonished each and every morning! Our family began to reconnect. Charlie remained a changed person, and everyone enjoyed the fruits of that.

I don't know why God did not answer this prayer for nine years, but I suspect it was to give me peace in the present with where Sam is currently. God has said, "Not yet" for Sam. But I have witnessed His power and healing love in other avenues and so I can rest in the fact that God is not ignoring us. He is not forgetting His beloved Sam. It is simply not the right time for reasons only He knows. I don't know that I could have reached that peace without seeing His miracles in other ways. I *know* what is possible, and so I can rest in where we are.

CHAPTER 12

Prayer Posture

I have found our good God to often be a God of "not yet." It seems to me that He is all about the journey. The deeper I have gone in my faith and the closer I have grown to my God, the more I have found Him to be utterly perplexing and frustrating, to be honest. The honeymoon is over, and things have gotten real. He seems to really enjoy leading me along paths to nowhere (or so it seems). But this makes sense to me. God is all about drawing you into a deeper surrender—and that can really only happen on the journey. And when you think you have surrendered as much as a person can possibly surrender, you will find that there are more levels still. Should God answer everyone's prayers instantaneously, the potential for growth would be only as deep as the level of surrender demanded of you. Long journeys demand tremendous growth.

Occasionally, prayers are answered instantaneously to bolster our faith. But I have found that this is not the way God deals with us for the most part. He knows that we are capable of more growth than what we are offering Him at this moment. I am typically not willing to even acknowledge the growth that I am capable of unless it is demanded of me, and I remain open to the long slow process of being molded. It has often felt like God has broken my heart again and again. Over and over. He leads me to long for a home for my heart but leaves me in the spiritual wilderness. He leads me to hope for restoration for my son but then doesn't deliver. In this breaking of my heart, however, I can see the fingerprint of God and my heart grows softer. I have come to expect nothing whatsoever and everything at the same time. Over time, I have become indifferent to God's timetable. I hope for something because He very often gives gifts, but I expect nothing specific because I have not once succeeded in figuring Him out. We tend to try to "figure God out," to feel confident that we know which way life is headed simply because He has spoken to us and told us it is going to be so. I'm not saying that God is lying. He will absolutely make sense of all He has promised us, but to presume to know exactly how God will fulfill His promises is an exercise in futility. We don't know until we know. When God breaks your heart, when He leaves expectations unfulfilled, when He draws you in and leads you down a path and then seemingly does an about-face and walks the other direction, we can sometimes feel abandoned. Or perhaps like we have judged wrongly. It all feels very confusing. We must realize that each time this happens, it is God who is saying, "Just keep going. You don't need to know how it ends. All I ask is that you trust me and surrender to wherever I may lead you." A virtual game of Follow the Leader. It has been my experience that clear direction and warm fuzzies are for those who St. Catherine says are at the 'heart of Jesus'—those who are still getting to know their God. He wants you to experience His love and His consolations. He wants to first lead you to trust Him completely. Once He has cap-tivated your heart, He begins leading you down paths of surrender for the good of your soul. These roads to nowhere, these about-faces, these perplexing journeys—they lead you to expect absolutely noth-ing other than what He wants to give you in that moment.

I believe God has promised me restoration of my son. But until it happens, it hasn't happened. I believe He will fulfill His promise in time, and so I'll leave my hand outstretched until He does so. The process of learning to accept unanswered prayers is a very painful process indeed. When I would take Sam to a healing service or find myself engrossed in prayer in my own home, begging my Heavenly Father for his healing, I would often find my request "ignored." Each time we took Sam to see Dr. Nemeh, and we experienced the healing love of God in so many different but tangible ways, and yet Sam's healing never came. Each time this happened, it took me a good day to recover from that. There was a lot to work through emotionally. It felt very much like my God, whom I loved so much, was breaking my heart again and again and again. This process was very much a part of my faith journey. If I could acknowledge that God had Sam in His hand at the moment of his affliction and in the hours, days, weeks, and months that followed…if I could clearly see His divine providence in how everything played out…if I was witness to God's physical and profound healing in my girls, then I had to acknowledge that the "no" or the "not yet" was also within God's perfect plan. I had to accept that Sam was exactly where God wanted him, even if it felt like He was ignoring our requests. If I trusted my God, then I had to trust my God in everything. No matter how long the road was. No matter if I "heard" Him or not.

After experiencing this broken heart again and again, I became better at accepting the outcomes. Growth happened. Eventually I was able to bounce back faster and then finally detach myself from the outcome altogether. I eventually learned to ask with a certain indifference to the yes or no. Hope in the yes but acceptance of the no. This is one example of the fruit and the growth of a long journey. Long journeys demand much, but the amount of growth can be substantial if we are willing to cooperate.

As we walked on Calvary with Sam, our entire life became a prayer. Every breath, every minute was a very grueling and exhausting cry to God. And so when we would receive advice on how to go about getting Sam healed, it was a very heavy burden to bear. It did not give me the freedom to simply be with my God. It did not allow me to cry but instead approached tears as a necessary evil to recover from in order to get back on track spiritually. Tears were seemingly the antithesis to positivity. The rate of burden that this added to our cross was substantial as I had to somehow earn His favor rather than resting in His arms. Though always well-intentioned, I received a good deal of advice concerning our prayer for the miraculous.

"Stay positive!"

"Claim your victory!"

"Make sure you are in the right frame of mind before you ask!"

"Try this or that…there is incredible power to be found if only you."

"Don't doubt!"

"Perhaps there is someone you haven't forgiven from your past."

I could go on and on. Here is what I know. While a negative and resistant attitude could very well frustrate God's hand on your life, while we can choose not to receive his healing (free will), God's gifts are not bound by our ability to work ourselves into a perfect frame of mind. If we have to work *that hard* in order to receive His gifts, then they are no longer gifts. They become something we feel we can earn. We run the risk of becoming superstitious in how we view God's mercy. If we metaphorically stand on our head and think good thoughts and account for every last little grudge we have ever held and say prayers to the right saint for this given situation and spin around three times and make sure there isn't even a sliver of doubt that our God *will* say yes and do the incredibly hard work of maintaining the proper positive mindset for the duration of the appointment or service or what-have-you—then and only then will He be favorable to us.

I'm exaggerating, of course, but I think it makes my point. God asks for very little. The slightest amount of faith and hope. A cracked door of hope for a Savior. Quite often—perhaps even most often— He says, "Not yet. There is still work to do." Whether or not He ever actually says no is above my pay grade. Even if He makes us wait until eternity for our healing, that would still fall under the category of "not yet." But I can say with a fair amount of certainty that "not yet" is quite often His response. But His denial of your request is not because you have not yet found the magic combination of how to approach Him. A heart turned toward Him is all He requires in order to hear us. All we can really do is ask and receive—nothing more.

This isn't to diminish the importance of faith or forgiveness. A hard heart could very well frustrate the gifts and the graces that our Lord wants to give us. Just as in the "Our Father," we pray, "Forgive us as we forgive others." We would be foolish to contentedly sit in our hatred of our neighbors and still believe that God will give us the desires of our hearts. He *can*. He can also heal the atheist in order to wake Him up. And He *does* do this from time to time. But understand that if you have even a little faith, God may be stretching you and asking for more. Do not be downhearted if your request seems to be denied. He just sees a tremendous amount of potential in you for growth and is asking you to simply surrender a bit more. And so yes. We should examine those areas where our hearts may be hard before asking for favors. A hard heart can be what stands in our way between our desires and God's graces. But I have found believers to sometimes be scrupulous in their approach to the Father, trying every which way to gain His favor. Standing on their heads to get His attention. *Be still.* Approach Him in humility. And ask. And then thank Him in anything and everything.

Such are the gifts from our Father. If the gift is to our detriment because we have no intention of growing in virtue or allowing our hearts to soften, then of course we could very well be denied our requests simply due to our stubborn nature. But on the flip side, we need not worry too much about doing enough to earn our Father's gifts. They are freely given, and He delights in giving them to us in accordance with His Holy Will.

Our prayers to the saints are another area in which there can exist a superstitious posture. This great treasure of the Church, the *Communion* of Saints, *can* be reduced to a group of talismans used in an attempt to manipulate God. Like collectors trading cards. "Did you try this one? How about that one? I've heard there is a lot of power in prayers to this one!" The nature of the Communion of Saints is one of, well, *communion!* We are brought together in union of heart with our holy brothers and sisters who have gone before us. We are to approach them as friends and enter into relationship with them as we approach our Father. Which saints are we drawn to? They may just be initiating a "conversation" with us. Who is the patron saint of our cause? Who is our own personal patron saint that we are named after? These are our friends whom we can ask to intercede for us and pray with us to our Father.

There *is* power in sacramentals and relics. Consider the handkerchiefs and aprons of St. Paul that brought healing to those who believed or Peter's shadow that cured those who fell under it. God *does* use His holy people and holy objects as vessels to bring about His healing. There *is* power in our prayers to the saints. There *is* power in the blessed articles that are in the treasury of our Church. There are even people and places here on earth where God has willed that heaven touch down and have become a portal to the miraculous. But where does this power come from? On the surface, we know that it comes from God, and yet sometimes we behave as if one saint has more or less power than another. Or that perhaps we simply haven't discovered the right cocktail of saints in order to gain God's favor. The power or healing that comes to us is both given and withheld by the same Lord. He always hears us regardless of which saints we have asked to pray for us. And He always has an answer. "Yes, no, or not yet."

This Communion of Saints is similar to any good friend here on earth. When you ask them for their prayers, they should ultimately point you toward God. Which of your friends, upon hearing that your prayer was answered, would say, "You're welcome. I did that"? The saints *are* powerful intercessors precisely because God has willed that we all participate in His saving work. He does not need them to distribute His graces, but in His goodness, He has determined that it is in our best interest if we get involved in the journeys of one another. He encourages us, as well as the saints, to be instruments of his love and mercy and power. All requests go to Him. All answers are given by Him. All glory belongs to Him—regardless of which Saint you have asked to pray for you and with you.

As I have sought healing for my son, I *have* remained positive. The door to my heart *has* remained wide open to receive God's graces. I *have* worked to forgive anyone who I felt had wronged me. I *have* confessed my sins to the extent that I have been made aware of them. And I have *no doubt*! I have moved beyond "faith in" to a "knowledge of" His power. I have witnessed the miraculous firsthand. I *know* what God can do and is willing to do! And yet Sam has not been healed. It is not dependent on our work. It is *His* gift to us to be gratefully received. Not demanded. Not presumed. Received. I stand before my Father as a little child with my hands outstretched, asking for whatever grace He is holding behind His back for me.

So just how long, exactly, should we persist in our request? At what point should we assume that God has said "no" and lay it down? Consider Luke 11. Remember the story about the guy who shows up at his friend's house at midnight asking for a loaf of bread? He is told to go away because everyone is already tucked in tight. But look at what happens when he is not deterred by the answer.

> *I say to you, though he will not rise and give to him because he is his friend, yet because of his persistence he will rise and give him as many as he needs. "So, I say to you, ask, and it will be given to you; seek, and you will find; knock, and it will be opened to you. For everyone who asks receives, and he who seeks finds, and to him who knocks it will be opened. If a son asks for bread from any father among you, will he give him a stone? Or if he asks for a fish, will he give him a serpent instead of a fish? Or if he asks for an egg, will he offer him a scorpion? If you then, being evil, know how to give good gifts to your children, how much more will your heavenly Father give the Holy Spirit to those who ask Him!"*

This is quite a promise! In this one example, we can learn that God desires that we pester Him, that we never give up hope. That we persist until we have "moved the heart of God," so to speak. Fr. Garrigou-Lagrange, O.P. in his book, *The Three Ages of the Interior Life*, calls this persistence and fortitude "limitless annihilation!" When it feels as if we are being ignored or even when we perceive to have been denied, it is the will of our God that we should continue to ask! And not just once more, He delights in our persistence in our "limitless annihilation!" I *love* that phrase!

Much is learned on the journey as we continue to hope in the face of disappointment. Out of concern for my heart, others have expressed that I should possibly "just be grateful for what we still have and lay down my hope for more." After all, how many times can one person have their heart broken? It would be easier on all concerned to just accept and move on. On one hand I would agree! It takes a lot of work to hope! A great deal of spiritual muscle is required to continue hoping when things seem bleak. In some regards, it would be far easier to just lay it down, accept what is, and move on. Except for one thing. My heart won't let me. And so, in that regard, to go against a hope that was planted there and nurtured by God Himself would be darn near impossible and would fall under the category of despair. Giving up. Stifling the Holy Spirit's work in my heart. No, I'll continue hoping and asking until I draw my last breath. If I ever do choose to lay it down, it certainly won't be because I am defeated or because I have given up hope in my God. Should I lay down my hope for Sam's healing, it would only be because my God has clearly expressed to me that it is His will that we should lay it down and embrace this cross for the duration. There will be peace…and grace…and closure. So long as He sends manna encouraging me to hope for more, that is what I should do.

Concerning the "just be grateful," there is a not-so-implicit suggestion in this expression that when one hangs onto hope for more healing, they are somehow failing to see the bright side of things, failing in their gratitude for the blessings they have already received. Hope and gratitude are not mutually exclusive virtues. There is no cognitive dissonance in holding onto both. I have found God to be a God of abundance, not a god of "good enough," not a god who rations his blessings. No! Our God is a God of plenty! When He multiplied the loaves and the fish, there was an abundance left over. When he healed the sick, He did so completely—and forgave their sins to boot! When He changed the water into wine at Cana, He saved the good stuff for the end of the celebration! It is not only possible to be grateful for His graces while still asking for more. It is, in fact, the proper posture. Hope does not mean living in denial of reality. Hope is not the defense mechanism of someone who can't accept their cross. Having faith in the promises of God means having *"confident assurance concerning what we hope for and conviction of the things we do not see" (Hebrews 11:1).* Even when our hope seems foolish in the eyes of the world, it is our work to continue in hope. Hope is hard work, but sometimes it is hard work to be a fool for God.

Going back to the above-mentioned lesson in Scripture where we consider that a father would never give his son a serpent rather than the fish he requested, we also learn that our Heavenly Father *will* answer our prayers! *"Ask and you will receive!"* That's quite a promise! He will not place in our hands something that can harm us when we have asked for a blessing. I would argue that occasionally, however, when we ask for a fish, He might give us a hamburger. Or when we ask for bread, he may give us pasta. We don't always receive the good thing we are asking for, but we can rest assured that He will always meet our needs and give us those things that are best for us. Maybe not the gifts we asked for, but tremendous graces nonetheless. And those gifts and graces *will* be the answer to our prayer. Perhaps not exactly the answer we were expecting, but an answer nonetheless. If we have not yet received an answer, we would do well to continue asking. How many graces never reach the hands of the faithful simply because they have given up? They have grown weary of asking. They assume God's perceived silence is a denial of their request! No! Continue to ask until you have received His answer. Persistence and fortitude in our prayer life leads to a considerable amount of faith and hope! And if you should at long last receive that hamburger instead of the fish you were craving, *then* you will have your answer, and *then* you can thank God for whatever good gift He saw fit to give you. And you will be able to rest in it. You will not need to relegate it to the category of prayers that have gone unanswered.

When God plants thoughts of hope in my heart for Sam's restoration, I take Him at His word, and so I continue to ask for that. Perhaps He means fully and completely and that it will happen tomorrow. Perhaps He means at the Resurrection, but He is leading me along paths of hope in this life for a specific purpose. Only time will tell.

One prophetic word that has already come true to a certain extent was given to me again and again, even early on when I didn't understand it. From the very beginning of Sam's emergence from his coma, even when he first began talking again, friend and stranger alike would periodically exclaim how Sam was "so smart!" I thought it to be an odd observation at first. Initially, he could barely talk let alone display his intelligence, and yet people noticed *something*. I saw his new slower processor, and others saw his potential. I saw his academic regression, and others saw an exceptional quality. Nurses, anesthetists, volunteers, Mrs. Nemeh, therapists, Dr. Masgutova—they all saw something that either I was not seeing or that was not yet so. But each time someone made mention of his intelligence, I would interiorly utter a "Huh" and place it in my pocket as a promise of good things to come. Indeed, we discovered in time that God did send his angels to watch over Sam's cognition. His memory is astounding! His wit is spot on! He did regress academically, but he is learning better now than he did the first time around! We have already been shown how God protected this part of Sam, but I also trust that we are still in the very early stages of cognitive recovery. It was only recently that I was able to look at the IQ score in his chart and brush it off because it is just not an accurate representation of Sam's potential. He is "so smart," I concur!

This journey quite often makes me weary. I ask God again and again for His healing touch because not only do I mourn for Sam and his struggles, but because I am plain tuckered out as well. This. Is. A. Long. Road. And there is no end in sight! For how much I value the journey, I will happily unburden myself of the work as soon as God sees fit. I would *love* for it to be taken out of my hands so that I can give myself no credit for any progress we make. Even until I draw my last breath, that is what I will ask for if that is where He leads my heart. I will put my heart out there again and again, knowing He can, hoping He will, accepting His answer. Hopeful surrender.

Concerning my journey into the wilderness and my homesick heart, I can say that it is a small thorn that still pesters me. To never feel the comfort of being home even when I am home, to have a heart that is nomadic and unable to put down roots, to wander spiritually in the desert is, in itself, a trial of sorts. But gratefully, the desert is beautiful and lovely. This wilderness is not too shabby. We have a beautiful home on a lovely piece of property. And I am with my family. All things considered, it is a very small cross. There are far worse trials. But the fruits of this cross can be found.

For one thing, because I am not attached to my location, it has freed me up to comfortably travel around the country seeking help for Sam. It has allowed me to easily disconnect from my location to spend a considerable amount of time with my family in Florida as we wait out the winter. Additionally, after walking the path of Calvary, I now live with one foot in heaven and the other on earth. This world has lost its luster. My homesick heart has become a spiritual metaphor for the reality that we are all simply passing through this world as our true home exists only in heaven. Perhaps God will lead my heart to experience that "Ah, I'm home" feeling while here, but if not, if my heart remains homesick, it is an excellent and constant reminder of where I am ultimately journeying to. Should He allow the thorn to remain, I will praise Him for it. I have felt homesick for years now. My oldest baby is approaching seventeen years old. Admittedly, the thought of God answering this prayer in a physical change of location at this point is met with more trepidation than Him allowing the thorn to simply remain. At this point, my Charlie has one foot out the door as he approaches adulthood. Most of our memories are now at this location. For God to choose to move us after all this time feels unsettling and late in the game. On the contrary, the old familiar thorn is, well, familiar. Nonetheless, I will let Him lead, and I will follow—anywhere or nowhere.

Surrender. Let go of all expectation. Expect only that God will continue working in your life in surprising ways. He *loves* to surprise us! God is not predictable, and to presume that we know what the gift is before we open it is most likely inaccurate. He does not lie, but He shows His complexity more and more as we grow closer to Him. The longer we journey with Him, the more He demands of us in the realm of complete surrender. For a Father to spoil His child by always giving him what he wants when he wants it or giving him what he is expecting, this would teach the child nothing and would likely produce an ungrateful spirit. God likes the journey. He likes the suspense because it is there that He can teach us. He seems to "enjoy" keeping us in the ellipses of life rather than rushing us to the periods. He knows that we are capable of far more than what we are offering Him at this moment and He most often draws that out of us by taking us on the longer roads. Occasionally, He does surprise us with the instant gratification of an answered prayer and those moments are a great boon to our faith. But both are necessary as we progress in our relationship. We need those spontaneous gifts lest we lost heart. And we need the long journeys to stretch us and mold us. Expect nothing but hope for everything.

Consider one of my favorite stories—the story of Joseph. Early on, God showed Joseph his future. Based on his dreams, he knew that his brothers would one day bow down to him. I would love to know his thoughts as God seemingly did an about-face in his life. He was sold into slavery by his own brothers and forced to contemplate God's revelation to him as the sun rose and set again and again from behind his prison bars. Eventually of course, after years had passed, God brought to fulfillment all he had promised Joseph. When famine swept the land, his brothers arrived in Egypt in search of sustenance and did, in fact, bow down to him just as his dreams foretold. God did not lie. His word did not return to Him void, but the journey was just as important as the fulfillment.

How about the most well-known example of a very long journey? God's chosen people, the Israelites, wandering in the desert. God could have led them directly to the Promised Land but instead chose to test them in the desert which led to mutiny, ingratitude, and idol worship, landing them in a whole lot of "time out." Eventually He fulfills His promise and leads them into the Promised Land, but not before completing the long forty-year trek through the wilderness that undoubtedly shaped them.

Journeys are important. Journeys are where the growth happens. If God becomes utterly perplexing and confusing to you, take heart. He see's amazing potential in you and is molding your heart, calling you to a deeper trust—a deeper surrender. Just hold His hand and keep walking, confident that He knows the way.

CHAPTER 13

Providentially Perfect

I have learned that some journeys are meant to be traveled in isolation. No matter how many people surround you, ultimately it is you that needs to do the work of the suffering. It does not matter if twenty others are suffering by your side for the same exact reason. Each person's experience of the suffering is a journey that must be undertaken by only that person in light of their relationship with God. Each person's experience of a (perhaps) common suffering is entirely unique.

As our families rallied around us offering spiritual support and tangible help and as friends would offer to support us in any way they could, it was very clear to me very early on that this was a road that, ultimately, I would need to travel on my own—hand-in-hand with my husband and children, of course. The experience felt very similar to labor and delivery. For the blessed event of bringing a life into the world, people could pray for our journey and offer meals, shower the baby with gifts, but ultimately the suffering was mine to go through. Nobody could labor and deliver my baby except for me. Only I could walk that road. Likewise, nobody could drink the chalice I was drinking in suffering for my son. Nobody could carry my cross for me. This isn't to diminish the support we received. I truly don't know how we would have made it through without the support of the body of Christ. But the suffering aspect, the mother's heart that had to break and survive—that role could not be assumed by anyone other than me. No amount of love or support could alleviate or diminish that journey. No amount of help could remove even a single step that I was being asked to take. In order to do the work, it was necessary that I isolate myself, for a time, even from those I was closest to. I was desperate for God. I was desperate for His guidance and His love. I needed to hear His voice and so I was very stingy with my time. So much of it was occupied with the hospital logistics that any quiet time I could manage was jealously guarded. Guarded and devoted to the work of suffering, to the work of grieving, to the work of trusting, and to the work of healing.

While in the hospital, I would sneak away to St. Bernard's in downtown Akron for Mass while Dave stayed with Sam. I remember sitting in the pew as glorious hymns were sung lifting the hearts of the faithful. It felt utterly contradictory to join in. "Hallelujah" felt almost as out of place as it would have if sung on Good Friday. I choked on it as I joined in with the congregation. It seemed altogether unnatural that life in general, that the world, should continue on as if normal when we were still very much at the foot of the cross.

As we said goodbye to the hospital and began our journey at home and as Sam achieved milestones and seemed to be "getting better," the world increasingly left us behind. That's what life does. We were, for the longest time, stuck in our crisis unable to join society. As we struggled month after month to barely stay afloat, life continued. Small talk and idle chitchat grated on me. Always and 100 percent of the time, Sam was at the forefront of my thoughts. While I was going through my day and attending to all that needed my attention, all of those thoughts occurred under the shadow of "Sam." Conversations with *anyone* about *anything* other than Sam was just too difficult for my brain to process. As we began gathering with family and cousins again, we just didn't quite seem to fit anymore. The relationships that were once very natural became labored and awkward. The cousins were as sweet as sweet could be and went out of their way to include Sam, but even in their sweetness and their inclusion existed a difference that was difficult to accept. Time with cousins is one of those familiar things that became painful simply because of its familiarity. The ease and casual play of years past contrasted against the careful, gentle, and calculated inclusion that now existed amplified the pain of the open wound. The old mold no longer fit.

For a while, admittedly, my preoccupation with our road created a very self-centered existence. It occurred to me from time to time that I simply stopped investing myself in or caring much about the world around me. I still couldn't tell you one thing that was going on in the lives of those I cared the most about. Every bit of my attention was focused on ourselves and our survival. And life went on. And people were "happy that Sam was so much better" and that "he was looking so good!" And we were stuck. At one point, more than a year post injury, I told Dave that I didn't feel like I was able to make an accurate assessment of where we were exactly. How "okay" are we? I couldn't be sure. I sensed that we were, in reality, more okay than I felt. But I couldn't be sure of that assessment. I was emotionally still clinging to the precipice and unable to fully comprehend that the danger had passed so that I could simply step down. I was completely incompetent in my attempts to assess the reality and severity of our present moment.

Even after all this time, God was still walking very closely with us and sending me the sustenance I needed to propel us forward. The necessary sustenance to maintain that hope in our hearts, to continue working toward more healing.

Sam's progress with therapy at the hospital all but stopped. We were sensing that our time with them was winding down. Around the same time, in February, Sam had his check-up with physiatry. At this appointment, Sam was asked, as usual, to remove his brace to walk down the hallway. We removed his shoes, his socks, and his brace as he attempted to stand up and walk. As expected, Sam's foot rolled completely on its side and turned inward in a violent spasm as he attempted to bear weight on it. After just a handful of steps, the good doctor called it off and told Sam he could put his shoes back on so as not to injure himself.

Against my better judgment, I asked the doctor his opinion on Sam's future. "In your opinion, do you think it at all likely that Sam will ever be able to either downgrade to a shorter brace or go without one altogether in time?"

Dr. Baird looked at me apologetically and shook his head. "I don't think so." He nearly gave me a glimmer of hope when he stopped short and said, "Well… I mean…," but then stopped again and went back to "No. It's not likely."

His words refused to stick. They bounced right off me as I began to consider all the new "outside-the-box" ideas I had been looking into. Rather than accepting the prognosis, I began wondering if we might be able to move Sam beyond prognosis on our own. I was ready to get to work.

We were preparing for our trip to Florida—the one I told you about at the beginning. The vacation that did not go so well for Sam. We needed to fly because Sam would not have survived the long drive. His patience was all of about five minutes long before the tears started. Hours in a car with the family would have been torture for all concerned.

All of the things we struggled with on that trip were quite significant. Folding in half to his left. Walking into walls. Drooling. Stuttering. Flat personality. Slow processor. Emotional outbursts. No patience. No coping skills. No peripheral vision to the right or to the left. Visual processing very sketchy. Impossibility of walking barefoot. Needing assistance during bathroom trips. Falling constantly. Virtually no protective mechanism when he fell resulting in injuries to his head and body. Things were still very rough after seven months of full-time therapy.

I purchased a book a couple weeks prior to vacation from Dr. Masgutova's MNRI method. Her work involves Neuro-sensory-motor Reflex Integration. Basically, she works to integrate our primary reflexes that we are all born with but may not be integrated for one reason or another including a neurological injury. She is a brilliant scientist who has devoted her life to working with children and adults with some very serious injuries. She takes people through exercises that move their primary reflexes up the continuum from pathological towards dysfunctional and finally towards the more functional end of the spectrum. She goes back to the hardware endowed to us by our Creator and begins establishing foundations all over again.

When Sam was emerging from his coma and presenting as a newborn infant, those observations were about to become very important as I considered new options to help Sam move forward. Traditional therapy made Sam strong, but it could offer us very little more. This paradigm shift in thought was going to propel Sam beyond his plateau. Sam was making brand new connections in his gray matter, forming and myelinating pathways from scratch in an attempt to heal and restore. I now had the tools to help him build those connections from the ground up. Tools to help bring order to the disorder in his brain as it was making sense of its new reality. I decided to bring my new MNRI manual on vacation to begin attempting to make sense of the exercises and implement them.

As I sat by the pool in Florida, I cracked open my book and began reading. The more I learned, the more confused I became. The more answers I found, the more questions I had. I contemplated calling the MNRI office, but I figured they would probably tell me to just take one of their classes or that I would need to have Sam attend one of their family conferences. This would require an investment of a minimum of hundreds of dollars all the way up to over $10,000 for the week-long conference. As my list of questions grew, I decided I had nothing to lose, and so I dialed the number hoping to speak with someone knowledgeable and patient with me. As it turns out, the lady on the other end of the phone was most delightful! Sally was her name, and she was beyond helpful! We spoke for around forty-five minutes as she very patiently answered all of my questions.

In that conversation, I discovered that, providentially, Dr. Masgutova's office was only thirty minutes away from where we were staying on our vacation! Of all the places in the world, her headquarters happened to be in sunny Orlando, Florida! Recognizing the hand of God, I called the office and set up an appointment for Sam to meet with none other than the very brilliant Dr. Masgutova for an assessment.

Entering the MNRI facility, we were greeted by a warm and gentle smile on the face of this kind Russian lady. She led us back to her assessment room and got to work right away. She asked nothing about Sam's history or his deficits. It did not matter for the work she was doing. Where he is, is where he is. His history has no bearing on her recommendations for exercises. Although she spoke English, her rapid assessment made all the sense of a Russian monologue to me. As someone recorded the assessment, she uttered a continuous stream of "hyper" this and "hypo" that. "Plus-plus" or "plus-minus." I left the assessment knowing very little more than when I arrived, but I was definitely intrigued and motivated by her enthusiasm in how much she felt she could help Sam progress. We received our home program from this meeting, and I now had just enough information to begin our work. I spent our remaining time in Florida familiarizing myself with the manual and decided to begin our exercises upon returning to Ohio.

March is when we returned home, and so March is when we began. With my very ignorant hands, most certainly working in a very clumsy manner, I followed the exercises as best I could. Within around a week, Sam's stuttering all but stopped! Enthusiastically, we kept going! For the seven months we spent in therapy, seeing very slow small gains, I will tell you that all of the progress that we made through MNRI happened in a matter of weeks to around a couple of months tops. And all through my very inadequate hands! We found that suddenly, we no longer needed to remind Sam to sit up straight rather than sinking to his left. He found center all on his own! He was sitting straight and tall. He no longer ran into walls. He no longer drooled. His processing speed was ramping up, and Sam began coming alive! His flat personality, his indifference to play, his depression was lifting like a cloud and being replaced by an incredibly playful and social Sam! Sam, in his essence, came back to us through this work! He became emotionally stable for the most part. His patience was improving. He was becoming the big brother we remembered as he began to play with his little brother again. After beginning segmental rolling on the floor, Sam's peripheral vision on the right opened up completely in only three days! He went from having absolutely no peripheral vision to complete restoration on the right side in just seventy-two hours! Unbelievable!

Probably the most exciting and tangible change (other than his personality) was that, as of July, Sam no longer needed his brace to walk around! We were told likely *"never,"* and we achieved a flat foot in only four months! That's a bit ahead of schedule! He could now feel the floor beneath his foot! The blades of grass between his toes! His calf muscle, which had been terribly atrophied, was beginning to plump up! My boy was barefoot!

I believe we saw just as much progress in those weeks of beginning MNRI as we had in the entire course of his seven months of therapy in the hospital. After some time, we began to plateau with MNRI as well and were growing weary of the hours of exercises each day, and so we decided to take a break from it for a time as I set my sights on the work of Anat Baniel and Dr. Moshe Feldenkrais. We are really just at the starting gate concerning all of these modalities. We have much more to learn, but they are all offering us hope and expectation beyond anything we have found in our area. There are brilliant minds across the country and world who truly understand the power of neuroplasticity when given the proper tools and information. They witness the impossible becoming possible on a daily basis in their work. It has been such an uphill battle to learn about and implement these modalities. Literally hundreds, if not thousands, of hours researching, finding, studying, learning, implementing all of this new information. The cost has been tremendous in both time and money. Some of it has been worthwhile, and the rest has fallen away. I've gotten better at discerning the snake oil from the real deal over time. Because of the toll it has taken on our family, both in the realm of time and finances, we would love to gather the very best ideas from around the country and bring them to our area to help Sam and our community at large. Hope is sorely lacking in the realm of neurological recovery in our area. We would love to bring the hope that we have found to our hometown and to share it with others.

Our journey has led us to cross paths with an incredible network of other pilgrims. Hundreds of people followed Sam's journey on Facebook and lifted him in prayer for months on end. Friends and strangers alike invested themselves in his progress. Professionals from the hospital and in the realm of therapy—some of whom we still maintain contact with, others who we now call friends. Patients we have met who we are now invested in. Priests and lay people who made themselves available to attend to our every spiritual need. The good people of MNRI and the Neurological Recovery Center and Dr. Nemeh's office. The angel in the waiting room at our PCP's office who gave up her appointment for Sam. Random chance meetings with key people in grocery stores and fast food restaurants who spoke inspired words to us. New friends who have already walked the same long road we are walking who have offered us support and friendship as we share a common story. The crosshatch pattern formed by all of these new points of contact over the past two years makes me incredibly curious as to the design of the Creator's hand. Once the tapestry of time is unrolled, and I am able to glimpse the threads that were ours and how they intertwined with the threads of those around us, only then will I be able to fully comprehend the impact of one person on another. And all of these new friends we have had the privilege of meeting and interacting with, they too have their own incredibly complex network of lives they have touched! It's truly mind-blowing to consider!

In the midst of all this work and through witnessing progress through our own effort and our own hands, I have always been anxious to participate in healing services as they were offered in our area. They have kept me grounded and humble. It is easy to get caught up in the mindset of "How can *I* help Sam?" and then to get excited about the work of *my* hands as we see improvement. The healing services are an opportunity to lay it down and ask for nothing other than the healing touch of God. It is also a good reminder that as I go about doing this work, that ultimately the restoration is up to God. It is God who tells the sea to go this far and no further. It was God who determined to what extent He would allow Sam's injury to progress, and it is God who will either frustrate or multiply the work of my hands. The healing services help me to keep God at the center of Sam's entire healing process throughout the hard work and to give Him the glory for all progress.

On one occasion, we took Sam to a service at St. Paul's Parish in Canton. It was a beautiful service, but nothing very significant took place in the realm of healing. However, when we arrived home and entered the house, I noticed that Sam smelled as if he had been anointed with baptismal chrism. It was a very strong sweet and musky smell. Very unmistakable. I smelled those around me. Nothing. Dave smelled my head. Nothing. I called my parents. They had not been anointed with oil either. Finally, I asked one of the volunteers from the evening, and she confirmed that no oil had been used on anyone at the service that evening! And yet our entire household could smell the heavenly aroma on Sam's head! He was anointed for the work before him—for the mission that was his. This was a God-wink letting me know that Sam was very much in the palm of His hand even though we are not yet receiving the healing that we are hoping for.

Around two months later, we traveled north to the Shrine of Our Lady of Lourdes. We strolled the beautiful property and filled our containers with the Holy Water. Looking up at the sky, Sam noticed the battle between the sunshine and the rain clouds that constantly vied for position as we walked. One minute, the rain seemed as if it would win out only to be replaced minutes later by a beautiful blue sky. It continued in this manner for the entire duration of our visit. Sam perceptively drew a parallel between the battle in the sky and the spiritual battle that was being waged.

As we made our way to the chapel to spend some time in prayer, we filed into the pew and knelt down. After a few minutes, I looked up and noticed the sunlight streaming through the "Mary Blue" stained glass windows. It poured down, focusing its beam on one particular target. It had landed on the head of Sam. As we prayed for a while longer, I turned my attention to the sunbeam again and again. As the sun moved through the sky, it poured through various positions on that window. The beam landed, all the while, on the battered head of Sam—a detail that was not lost on our entire group of prayer warriors. Love notes and forget-me-nots.

Once we were home from our vacation and beginning our work outside of mainstream therapy, we had some pretty good momentum going in the line of progress. Surprising progress, in fact. Unfortunately, a pretty big wrench was thrown into our plans after we visited Sam's neurosurgeon, Dr. Chen. We were concerned about the way his head looked to us. She confirmed our suspicions that something was awry. Sam's skull was disintegrating. Apparently, there is a high probability that a skull will resorb once it is replaced in the body. The longer it remains outside of the body in a freezer, the more likely the replacement will be unsuccessful. His skull had been in that freezer for a good couple months before returning to its home in Sam's head. As the skull bone began to resorb, it was leaving pockets and holes. Some areas were clear through the bone and others left only a very delicate sheet of bone that you could most likely put your finger straight through with only a little effort. Sam would need to go under the knife once again. They needed to replace the entire right half of his skull bone with a plastic plate. One more surgery on his poor head loomed in his future. My spirit resisted going down this path, but we had no choice.

The day prior to his surgery, my spirit was restless. As I looked in the sky, however, I was reassured by a single small cloud that remained in an otherwise completely clear sky. I felt confident that this was one final major blip on the radar that we must endure before moving on. Mercifully, God must have anesthetized my conscious-ness during the whole ordeal. I mean, I know I was there, and I even recall a couple positive pieces of the experience, but overall, I really have no recollection of most of those days. I know there was surgery. I know there was swelling. I know we spent time in the hospital—ports, drains, staples, and stitches. I just really don't remember any of it. I *do* remember Dr. Chen telling me how pleased she was that when she opened Sam back up, she found a beautifully reformed dura layer—a beautiful dome beneath his skull! Apparently, that doesn't always happen and was a very positive thing for his recovery. Thank the Lord for domed dura matter! Who knew?

Despite this major surgery and despite Sam's fractured arm from a bad tumble and despite spending time in the hospital for a seizure that occurred when trying to wean Sam from his medication, it was, nonetheless, during this time that we witnessed the rapid progress through our new therapies despite these setbacks.

By and by, as time marched on and the gains were hard won, we entered a period of time when we were seeing very little progress and feeling a bit defeated at the deficits that remained, I received a sur-prise message from a nurse who works at Children's Hospital but also attends our church. It spoke of the miracle that *is* Sam and helped me to put the remaining deficits in perspective.

Hi, Pam.

I just wanted to reach out to you because Sam has been on my mind this weekend, and I wanted to share my experience. On Sunday, our team was speaking with the neurosurgery team, and we were discussing what a miracle it is when a patient survives a ruptured AVM. The neurosurgeon was describing the perfect storm that has to occur for a patient to survive without neurological devastation. In order to survive, a patient must arrive at a Children's Hospital when a neurosurgeon is in house (meaning they are physically present at the hospital at the time of presentation. Typically, patients present in the off hours when the surgeon has to come from home), with an OR suite ready to go and an anesthesia team in house and ready to go. This neurosurgeon pointed out how it is a one-in-a million chance this even happens. Then out of her mouth came what we were all already thinking, "Like the time Sam Lile presented to our hospital with those exact circumstances! It never happens! But it did for him." I was telling Gwen that when I see him at church, my thought is always that he is a walking miracle. Everyone agreed because you just never see anyone survive a ruptured AVM like Sam did without neurological devastation. I just had to share because non-pediatric medical people may not appreciate in the same way what a miracle Sam is. In the hard days at work, reflecting on the miracles is what gets you through. I am sure your family has hard days at home on his path to recovery. Please know it is a miracle straight from God that he is

*with you. I'm sure you already know that. Hope you
are all doing well.*

As we considered the miracle of Sam's gentle entrance into this
world all those years ago and how we were home from vacation when
he went down; as we contemplated how Dave was home, how I was
home, how Sam was not outside playing by himself, how we did not
send him to bed to sleep it off, and how he went down right at our
feet, we *knew* of God's providence and protection in how it all played
out. We knew it was miraculous that he was still with us based on
the sequence of events at home. We had no idea, however, that it was
equally miraculous on the part of the hospital. It did not occur to us
that instant access to surgery was a rare luxury. Miraculous indeed!
Sam still has work to do in this world, and we can rest assured that
Sam is exactly where he is supposed to be. How utterly ungrateful
and ignorant to claim that God's hand was on him at the moment of
his crisis but that He has now abandoned him and left his healing to
hard work and to chance. No. God *was* with him. God *is* with him.
God *will be* with him. Every inch of this is within God's holy will.
The prayers, the work, the setbacks, the victories, the glitches, the
joy, the pain, the celebration, the sorrow. It is all completely within
His will, and He *will* use every bit of it!

In order to understand the process of healing in my own heart,
I want to share a story about an important realization that took place
in October. It was Sam's tenth birthday, and I found myself caught
unaware by that old pal grief that tends to just show up unannounced.
It was the day after his birthday, and by all accounts, Sam was really
doing quite well. But I found myself entirely beat up. I lacked the
resolve to leave my bed or engage with my world, which led to a
considerable amount of introspection. What I realized through this
experience is that it was time to let go of our past and instead look to
the future. You see, emotionally, it was as if someone had come into
my home and vandalized it—uprooting everything, ripping things
away from me that I loved, leaving my home in complete disrepair. I
had spent the past year and a half desperately trying to restore what
was lost. I have been cleaning, dusting, sorting, painting, placing

things lovingly back up on the shelves, working so hard to recover what was lost.

But then, on this tenth birthday, I suddenly looked up, and I realized that I had been focusing so long on the pieces and parts, the details of my home, that I didn't even notice that it is now a different structure altogether. The house I loved, the one I was working so hard to restore, no longer exists. I can't go back to it. We now live in a completely new and different house, and I am holding onto a vision that can never be. You see, Sam is ten years old now! He was only eight when he had the hemorrhage. He is a different person. I am a different Pam. Dave is a different Dave. We are a different family than the one that existed in 2018. There is no going back. Time has marched on. It is not possible to return to the little boy in my memories. He is nearly two years older, and even if he hadn't suffered a stroke, he would still be a different person now than the boy in my memories. Even if he is completely 100 percent restored, he would still be a completely different person. He is growing up. The eight-year-old Sam of the past is no more. He has become a new creation.

It took me a day to nurse that rip of the Band-Aid, but ultimately, I think it was an important realization—a healthy orientation. The only thing that matters now is who he is and who he will become. We are all works in progress, and the important work for all of us is to prayerfully utilize our minutes in light of the best selves we hope to become. Our destiny does not lie in the past. Sam is a new creation day by day, as we all are. It is not fair to him that I maintain a longing for who he was. This is who he is, and he is exactly where God wants him in this moment. With much gratitude, I can say that we have recovered a good portion of what was lost. Sam, in his essence, has returned to us. When we are able to let go of recreating our past, it is much easier to find our gratitude for the present and hope for the future.

In the course of events, I became friends with Cleveland's own, Trapper Jack. I was first introduced to him through his podcast *Blind Faith Live* as he chronicled the miraculous testimonies coming from the office of Dr. Isaam Nemeh. His words were music to my ears during a time when I really needed to believe in miracles. After a while, I invited him to my Parish as a guest speaker. It was such a hit that he returned just a few months later. We came to converse from time to time, and so as I was writing this book, I decided to send him a draft for some feedback. Providentially, the ideas presented in this book were coinciding with the thoughts of his own mind, and so he invited me to be interviewed for his new podcast *Touched by Heaven.*

Our conversation really centered around a handful of ideas from this book. We began by examining that conversation with God when He asked me if I would take the place of my father who was suffering a new cancer diagnosis. I have wrestled with that conversation from time to time over the past couple years. Would God really ask such a thing of me? Additionally, I now struggled with the "guilt" of my consent which seemingly ushered in tremendous suffering for Sam. And finally, I wrestled with the sacrifice that I was able to offer in my unborn baby. As I now hold my Henry Alexander in my arms and enjoy his smiles and giggles, it is unfathomable to me that I should have found offering him up to be in any way different than any one of my other children. A bit of confusion and even a smidge of guilt shrouded this otherwise peace-filled conversation with God. It was a conversation that I had truly wrestled with for close to two years but had never wanted to look at too closely due to the confusion that surrounded it. But as Trapper invited me to go further into this experience, I was finally able to examine it from all sides and to make peace with it. As I allowed myself to journey back into those minutes, I realized that in this "would you take his place" conversation with my God, there was no fear. There was no anxiety. There wasn't even the consideration that my "no" might mean certain death for my dad. It did not in any way feel as though the life of my father hung in the balance of my response. There was no smiting God demanding one sacrifice in exchange for another. On the contrary, the entire conversation was very peaceful and gentle. Had I sensed any anxiety or fear, I would have run in the opposite direction. No, this was purely a conversation between two friends. I was caught off guard and surprised by the question itself, but there was no fear of the Person asking. I have come to understand that God was simply asking me to examine my level of trust and surrender. Almost like you could put the word *hypothetically* before each of the questions. "Hypothetically, Pam, what would you say if I were to ask you to surrender everything?" There was no wrong answer. My God was simply helping to reveal myself *to* me. The only condemnation or judgement was my own as I realized the lack of trust in my responses. But there was no disappointment from my God. He already knew the answer I was going to give. They were *my* words, and it was *my* consent, but it was God Himself who asked questions of me that He already knew the answers to in order for me to learn more about my level of surrender.

Even my curious ability to surrender my unborn son caught my attention, it seems so irrational now. And I have come to see that it truly *was not* a rational response, but rather it was a *super*-rational response! It was a Holy Spirit response! Essentially God asked, "Would you be willing to give me everything?" And then He led me to offer what amounted to a cracked door of surrender.

And God assured me that this was sufficient. A cracked door was all He needed to work in my heart. Just a little surrender to allow Him admittance in order to begin His work in me.

"That will do" was His reply.

Where I first saw a clear delineation between what Jesus asked and what I responded has now morphed into a portrait where my God—through pointed questions—was revealing *to* me the beginning of my will to surrender. It was a springboard to begin the process of placing everything into His loving hands and surrendering everything and everyone to Him as I was about to be asked to trust Him as never before. As I recall the conversation, I clearly remember "the conversation ending as I walked out of the church." But the reality is quite different! That was merely the *beginning* of the conversation, and it is still ongoing even today!

Could the merits of my surrender and our suffering have had a direct and positive impact on the health of my father? Well, of course it is possible. In the mystical Body of Christ, our suffering is redemptive. It does have a positive effect on the entire Body in ways that we can't possibly understand this side of heaven. And so yes, it could be entirely likely that there exists a direct causal relationship between my surrender and my dad's health, but that was not the main component of the conversation. The entire gravity of the conversation was not wrapped up in the destiny of my father. The gravity of the conversation was completely about opening the door to surrender, taking our relationship to that next level. I have made peace with this very difficult question. I have found the love of God in the question, and I am so grateful for the experience as it was a call to something deeper than I had been experiencing. This conversation in church that day ushered in suffering, but it also ushered in unfathomable blessings, deep surrender, and the sweet kisses of my friend Jesus.

CHAPTER 14

Blessed Be the Name of the Lord

As I sat on the couch next to Sam, we meandered through his photo album containing all of our memories, both good and bad, throughout this long and difficult journey. I had just listened to my interview with Trapper Jack. Trapper had drawn a parallel between the consent to the sacrifice of both the Father and the Son, the consent of both Abraham and Isaac, and finally, the consent of Pam Lile when God asked her to surrender her children. The consent was a two-way street in each of these situations. It occurred to me, though, that the sacrifice was ultimately Sam's, not mine. Sam did not hear this conversation between Trapper and I nor did he know my thoughts as he sat there looking at his album. He paused briefly as tears filled his eyes.

When I asked what was bothering him, he struggled to express how he was just missing everyone and everything from his time in the hospital. Sam has complete and total amnesia concerning any negative aspects of his journey, and there were plenty of negative aspects, I can assure you! But he remembers none of it! Pureed foods, thickened liquids, hours of therapy, stuck in bed, pokes and prods, incredibly hard work—every bit of it is remembered with a sense of nostalgia. Sam proceeded to ask a hypothetical question. "What if we could go back in time and I knew that I was going to have a stroke, and I could tell you that it was going to happen?"

"Now *that* would have been very useful information." I chuckled.

Sam became quiet for a moment. Thoughtfully, he replied, "I wouldn't have told you."

As I pressed a little further, it was clear that Sam was consenting to his cross. Just as the Son did. Just as Isaac did. Sam, too, has embraced this difficult road that God has called him to. He does not count the cost of the cross. He only sees the blessings of it. As I gently nudged the conversation forward in contemplating even the difficulties that still remain and all the struggles he must continue to endure, he even went so far as to say that even now, even in these continued struggles, He would still do it again. He still considers it all worth it in the end. Consent to the cross, indeed he has.

We have returned to Florida once again. A year has passed since I began writing. When I set out to put our story on paper, I expected that by the time I reached my final chapter, I would have experienced an ending of sorts. A happily ever after, if you will. You know those long journeys we were just discussing? Well, this…*this* is a *very* long journey. We are nearly two years post injury. We are still praying, still hoping, still working, still asking how He wants us to use our experience. I can't say if we are near the fulfillment of its purpose or only in the middle. That is not for me to know. At least not yet.

We journeyed south this winter at the very last minute for a few reasons. Of course, R&R in the Florida sunshine is reason enough, but first, we headed to Texas for some unconventional therapy. We have been traveling the United States to find more hope-filled minds willing to propel Sam further. We are still in the beginning stages of exploring some of these options, but they are showing tremendous potential. We have felt called to bring some of these very good ideas home in order to help our community and we are just waiting on God to put the pieces together and to bless the project. We left Texas with hope in our hearts and a plan in place to begin fundraising as soon as we returned home. But first, we planned to spend the next three weeks in the Florida sunshine before returning home to get to work.

It is now March of 2020. As we sit in the sunshine and splash in the pool, the entire world has begun closing its doors for the Covid-19 pandemic. Nation by nation, state by state, no more school, no more public gatherings, no more church, no more toilet paper on the shelves of grocery stores—the entire global population severed from one another. Uncertainty permeates conversations as the world turns to social media and their trusted news sources in order to make sense of what is happening. Oddly enough, I find myself undisturbed. I mean, we are sitting in the sun by a pool, and so it is hard to take much of anything seriously. But it is deeper than that. I just can't seem to be disturbed by the news. I have been to hell and back, and so I think that builds a certain resilience. But as I examine the reason for my peace, I have come to understand the place we now find ourselves.

If you'll remember the beginning of my story a whole year ago, we were in Florida at that time too. Sam was not yet Sam. There was a tremendous amount of grief that I still needed to work through. But there was also a considerable amount of healing that was still to come as well. As we sit by the pool this year, our Sam who is now straight and strong, is no longer leaning, drooling, or stuttering with a processor that is now pretty darn fast and a memory like that of an elephant! We marvel at the fact that he has spent six straight hours playing in the pool. He is soaking up this vacation and enjoying the relaxation and play. He is emotionally stable. He loves the water. He loves to converse with any willing soul. He loves the sunshine and fresh air. We do not need to talk him out of his sweatpants and into summer clothes. He emerged from his room today barefoot and walking without assistance. He had gotten himself dressed after using the bathroom independently. He brushed his own teeth and combed his own hair. There are still some major disabilities that we are dealing with. He has, at this point, virtually no use of his left hand. Sand is his nemesis. When tired, his foot rolls pretty good, and walking is still labored and exhausting for him as he still leads with his left toe rather than his heel. Additionally, his visual field is pretty rough. But praise God, those are just details. This new creation is worth celebrating because in his essence, Sam was restored to us. Sam is alive. Sam is soaking up life and is a very happy boy. He does not count the cost of his injury. He just moves forward with little thought of what he left behind. He can only see the blessings of his journey with very little thought at all to the weight of the cross. Manna is still falling from heaven offering more hope, telling me to continue the journey, to continue the hard work, to expect more restoration.

We are currently expecting baby number nine. As I reflect on this amazing gift, I realize how much we were spared. I realize how much healing has taken place in a year. I realize that there was a time when the thought of another baby would have driven me to despair, and I notice how, not only are we not afraid, we are actually quite elated to welcome this little bundle into our lives. The whole family is very much looking forward to this blessing! If we can look forward in joy and without trepidation to a new baby, we *must* be in a better place. The kids are playing together in the pool. Dave is more amazing by the day. The patience that is now his, the contentment in his spirit, the playfulness that has returned as he engages with the kids, the light that has returned. Yes, this journey has been good for us. We have been sustained as we have traveled the very difficult road of Calvary, and we are now experiencing His resurrection incrementally as we limp towards brighter horizons.

As I write this final chapter, I am contemplating two crosses at once. Our own personal cross and the resurrection we are experiencing to some degree but also the global cross of this pandemic. Trials and crosses are a very unpopular notion these days. Many Christians are unable to reconcile the love of God with a deliberate cross or trial. Love and happiness are from God. Pain and suffering are from satan. Period. All crosses are viewed as an evil to be delivered from as people refuse to acknowledge the hand of a loving God in them. Are crosses and trials, in reality, antiquated Old Testament perceptions of our God? I think we would do well to remember that the God of the Old Testament and the God of the New Testament are the same God! God does not change. In fact, Jesus Christ makes the suffering we endure so much more understandable when we contemplate it in the light of His Cross and Resurrection! One only needs to look to Jesus Christ to find the love of God within the cross.

Everything that happens in this life—*everything*—passes through the fingers of God. We are not at the mercy of satan. Satan did not get the upper hand, and we are just waiting for God to finally win the war. No. Every little thing that blesses and afflicts us is known by and allowed by our loving Father. A Church that shuns the cross because it doesn't "feel" like a loving thing for our God to do is missing the whole point of the Gospel. The way to the Father is through Jesus Christ—through His cross, through His suffering, His death, and ultimately His Resurrection. That is life on earth in a nutshell! We walk the valley, uniting ourselves with Christ so that we can experience His victory! God does allow trials specifically to lead us to the Resurrection! These crosses are some of the greatest gifts that He has given us. They come to us from the hands of a loving Father who knows how to bring about the greatest good in our souls. If we can look at every tiny little thing in life through the lens of eternity, we will see that it *all* points towards that reality! The joy gives us a foretaste of what awaits us. The pain beckons us to cry out to our Savior. The trials allow us, through grace, to share in His Divine nature. Every bit of it works for the good of our souls. If we can approach every situation from this perspective, then we will see no evil. We will give satan credit for nothing that happens in our lives. All glory will be given to God for the joys as well as the sorrows, and we will see the beauty of His hand in everything. And we will grow to love Him more even through those crosses.

Some crosses are short and fierce. Others are the equivalent of a long dull pain. Some are temporary and others, sadly, are permanent this side of heaven. I am sure there is an altogether different learning curve concerning the very deep and lasting suffering of someone handed the very permanent cross of the death of a loved one—especially those victim souls who have lost a child or those who have found peace in their acceptance of a very difficult cross that is far more life-altering than the one we are dealing with. Their fidelity to their Lord in the midst of such suffering is creating the most glorious strands of silver and gold in His grand tapestry and is most assuredly having a profound impact on the Body of Christ. No doubt that once they have completed their journey in this valley of tears, never abandoning their God, He will smile and say to them, "Well done, my good and faithful servant."

While walking through the fire with Sam, I found myself contemplating the story of Job. He was a devout and holy man who God allowed to suffer greatly. No matter what cross or trial God allows in our lives, I think we would do well to consider the response of this humble man. A contrite heart that continues to praise the name of the Lord, a contrite heart that acknowledges that it is all within the loving plan of his Father.

> *Then Job arose and tore his robe and shaved his head and fell on the ground and worshiped. And he said, "Naked I came from my mother's womb, and naked shall I return. The Lord gave, and the Lord has taken away; blessed be the name of the Lord."*
>
> *In all this Job did not sin or charge God with wrong.*

I think it is equally important to remember, however, that God never asks us to walk Calvary alone. While suffering tremendously, I found God to be very near. And very sweet. And very gentle. He consoled me in ways that are tremendous treasures to me and that will carry me forward my entire life. He demanded much of us, but all the while He united Himself to us with each and every step we took. In the end, He gave us far more than He ever demanded of us. The good that came from the journey cannot be measured. I don't think I could go so far as to say that I would choose the cross again if given the option. It's been rough, and I am human, but acknowledging that it was a gift from my God who loves me, I can say that the graces have been tremendous, and I do praise Him for every bit of it. We are currently still in the middle of the journey, but the graces from the trial have not yet been exhausted.

> *Blessed is the one whom God corrects;*
> *so do not despise the discipline of the Almighty.*
> *For He wounds, but He also binds up;*
> *He injures, but His hands also heal.*

If you have not read the book of Job, spoiler alert. God ends up blessing him in the end more than all the days before. There is *always* a Resurrection for God's people. We should pray for and hope for and expect that Resurrection. But while we are walking the road of Calvary, groaning under the weight of the cross, we must rend our garments, turn our hearts to the Lord, allow Him to speak to us and mold us, and praise Him all the while. We blame God for no evil. But we praise Him for even this and thank Him for His coming salvation. It is easy to praise God when the road is smooth and easy. The real test of our loyalty and love can be found when the terrain is rough and downright hard.

"Will you still praise me in those minutes?"

"Am I still your God? Or will you abandon me when I remove my hand of blessing?"

Are we, in the end, merely fair-weather friends or are we true disciples of the Living God? We must do the work of turning our hearts toward God while times are good so that we will know where to find Him when suffering comes our way. When life gets dark and it is hard to see much of anything, we need to be so familiar with Him that we can recognize His hand in the midst of our suffering.

No matter what this world throws at us, it is ultimately in this truth that we can find our hope. No matter what, we win! We know the end of the story. Whatever suffering we endure, whatever crosses we carry, whether our afflictions are temporary or "permanent," at the end of this life, we win! We are sometimes granted a taste of this eternity when our Lord chooses to send healing to our wounded and suffering bodies—and it is good to ask for these things—but we must understand the healing for what it is. It is a taste of our eternity! It is miraculous and amazing and wonderful, but in the end, it is merely a glimpse of our destiny! A glimpse of eternity where healing and health and joy and peace and comfort will be ours forever and ever! Living through Him and with Him and in Him, death will no longer be able to touch us. Suffering will no longer be able to grip us. And that is ultimately what our entire journey points us toward. The joy, the suffering, the healing, the pain—every bit of it points to the reality of this fleeting world and the permanency of our heavenly home. Every bit of it is to mold us and shape us so that we can, through adoption, share in His Divine nature! So that we can partake in His Resurrection!

"And after you have suffered a little while, the God of all grace, who has called you to His eternal glory in Christ, will Himself restore, confirm, strengthen, and establish you" (1 Peter 5:10).

As the world writhes and groans all around us under the weight of this pandemic, all I can see in lovely Florida is that life is good. And time changes things. And God does sometimes allow crosses and afflictions but only out of His love and goodness. And there is *always* a resurrection for those who love Him, and I think this is the reason for my peace. My happily ever after was found, after all, in the *middle* of our journey. We are *okay*. Sam is *okay.* The world is *okay.* It is well. It is well with my soul.

THE PLAN OF THE MASTER WEAVER

Our lives are but fine weavings
That God and we prepare,
Each life becomes a fabric planned
And fashioned in his care…

We may not always see just how
The weavings intertwine,
But we must trust the Master's hand
And follow His design,

For He can view the pattern
Upon the upper side,
While we must look from underneath
And trust in Him to guide.

Sometimes a strand of sorrow
Is added to His plan,
And though it's difficult for us,
We still must understand

That it's He who flies the shuttle,
It's He who knows what's best,
So, we must weave in patience
And leave to Him the rest…

LEAD ME LORD

Not till the loom is silent
And the shuttles cease to fly
Shall God unroll the canvas
And explain the reason why—

The dark threads are as needed
In the Weaver's skillful hand
As the threads of gold and silver
In the pattern He has planned.
(Author unknown)

ABOUT THE AUTHOR

Pam Lile, with an insatiable hunger for divine directives, has shared her incredible journey of faith. While suffering alongside her son, who endured a massive brain hemorrhage at the age of eight, she recognized early on that her family was in the midst of a beautiful story that God Himself was the author of. This most recent and painful chapter of her life has been a thorn amongst the roses that she has been blessed with. Pam resides in Ohio with her husband and nine beautiful children. Always ready to follow the prompting of the Spirit, Pam and Dave have embarked on many adventures, laying them all down for the most important work of their lives—advocating for their brain-injured son. Between diapers, laundry, and schoolwork, Pam enjoys reading, researching, and implementing advances in neuro-rehabilitation, and dabbling in her very mediocre garden.

CPSIA information can be obtained
at www.ICGtesting.com
Printed in the USA
FSHW011250020421
80104FS